Write Your Legal Will in 3 Easy Steps

Write Your Legal
Will in 3 Easy Steps

Tom Carter, Lawyer

Self-Counsel Press
(a division of)
International Self-Counsel Press Ltd.
Canada   USA

*Self-Counsel Press acknowledges the financial support of the Government of Canada
through the Canada Book Fund (CBF) for our publishing activities.*

Printed in Canada.

First edition: 2001 (3); Reprinted: 2004
Second edition: 2005; Reprinted: 2006
Third edition: 2008; Reprinted: 2008 (2); 2010 (2); 2012 (3); 2014

Library and Archives Canada Cataloguing in Publication

Carter, Tom (G. Thomas), 1950-

    Write your legal will in 3 easy steps/Tom Carter. — 3rd ed.
(Legal series)
ISBN 978-1-55180-801-7

    1. Wills—Canada—Popular works. 2. Estate planning—Canada—Popular works. I. Title. II. Series: Self-counsel legal series
KE5974.Z82C37 2007   346.7105'4   C2007-905777-2
KF755.Z9C37 2007

Self-Counsel Press
(a division of)
International Self-Counsel Press Ltd.

North Vancouver, BC   Bellingham, WA
Canada   USA

Contents

Estate Planning for Life: The Law of Aging

Your Enduring Power of Attorney

Your Advance Directive

Basic Will and Worksheets
103

Tables

CD Content
130

Notice

Laws are constantly changing. Every effort is made to keep this publication as current as possible. However, the author, the publisher, and the vendor of this book make no representation or warranties about the outcome or the use to which the information in this book is put and are not assuming any liability for any claims, losses, or damages arising out of the use of this book. The reader should not rely on the author or the publisher of this book for any professional advice. Please be sure that you have the most recent edition.

Note: The information contained in this book does not apply to the province of Quebec.

Preface

Over and over again you, our readers, tell us you want a wills book that is simple and straightforward. Lawyers tell us that there is no such thing as a simple will because every person's situation is different and those differences must be taken into account.

I practiced law for 20 years and during that time I prepared many wills for ordinary people with ordinary assets — people with children or grandchildren, jobs, houses, cars, insurance, and who were saving for retirement. However, my clients did not own holiday villas in exotic locations nor were they owners of large multinational corporations.

As I met with these people, discussed their needs, and prepared their wills I saw that the final products usually had a great deal in common. Of course there is no such thing as a one-size-fits-all will and each will I prepared did require customization to suit the specific needs of each client, but the overall structure of these wills remained very much the same.

My experience convinced me it was possible to write a book aimed at intelligent readers of typical means who wanted good information on how to prepare their own wills. Self-Counsel Press agreed with me and they published my first book about wills, *Wills Guide for Canada*, in 2001.

Wills Guide for Canada sold 60,000 copies and the second edition — renamed *Write Your Legal Will in 3 Easy Steps* — was published in 2005, which sold another 40,000 copies. These are exceptional numbers in the Canadian book publishing industry, which tells us that we got it right.

Now we offer you this third edition which keeps the "3 Easy Steps" approach and adds one more to make sure you sign and witness your will properly and to offer some tips on how to store your will safely.

The following are the 3 Easy Steps (Plus One):

- Step 1: Choose Your Executor
- Step 2: Categorize Your Property
- Step 3: Distribute Your Property
- Plus One: Sign, Witness, and Store Your Will

Of course, we continue to provide you in-depth information on key issues, and answers to your most frequent questions, in the resources section at the back of the book.

As an intelligent reader, you know that no book can substitute for good, personalized legal advice from your own lawyer. If you have any questions about your own particular situation, and you do not have a good lawyer that specializes in wills, the section called "Finding and Using a Good Wills Lawyer" will help you find one in your area.

Thank you to all of the 100,000 wonderful readers who made *Wills Guide for Canada* and *Write Your Legal Will in 3 Easy Steps* so successful. We are glad you found the books useful. For those of you who still haven't done your will, we hope that this edition will help you do just that.

How to Use This Book and CD

As you can see, the CD contains two wills: a Basic Will for people who do not need to appoint guardians for minor children and an Advanced Will for people with children for whom they wish to appoint a guardian and an alternate guardian. Before starting your will, choose the version that applies to you.

Then follow these simple steps:

1. Read Step 1: Choose Your Executor and refer to the relevant materials in Resources for answers to your questions. Decide who will be your executor (and alternates) and select the executor clause that works best for you from the CD called Step 1: Choose Your Executor Clauses. Insert the appropriate clause into your will.

2. Read Step 2: Categorize Your Property and refer to the relevant parts of the Resources section for answers to any questions. Then complete Step 2: Categorize Your Property to identify the assets that pass under your will and those that do not.

3. Read Step 3: Distribute Your Property and, again, refer to the relevant sections of the Resources to answer any questions. Then choose the appropriate distribution clause from Step 3: Distribute Your Property Clauses (available on the CD) and insert it in your will.

4. Read Plus One: Sign, Witness, and Store Your Will then print your will, sign, witness it properly and store it safely.

I have also included samples of two other important estate management documents, the Advance Directive (also known as a Living Will) and the Enduring Power of Attorney. Unlike your will, these documents allow you to appoint someone to make health care decisions for you and to manage your financial affairs if you become incapable of doing so during your lifetime. To help you prepare these forms I have included the Enduring Power of Attorney and Advance Directive Planner.

If you have any problems understanding the legal terms used in this book, the CD includes a Glossary of common legal words defined.

Finally, on the CD I have included a number of forms and information lists you may wish to complete for your executor to help make his or her job easier when you die:

- Checklist (for what to do when a death occurs)
- Contents of House (to help you list what will go to the beneficiaries)
- Money Owed to Me (lists the debts owed to you)
- People to Contact (list of friends, professional and religious advisors, etc., to contact at the time of death)

- Property and Real Estate (lists all property and real estate owned at time of death)

- Storage of Documents (includes information of where the executor can find your important documents and information about your funeral wishes)

- Storage, Safety Deposit Boxes, and Safes (includes the locations and where to find the keys or combinations to these important places)

- Vehicles and Vessels (includes all the information needed for these assets)

Choose Your Executor

The person in your will who is in charge of finding your assets, paying your debts, and distributing your estate is called the executor. He or she has a very important job to do, and because you won't be around to make sure your executor does it properly, you need to choose the right person for the job. You need someone who is able and available to act as executor when the time comes and he or she has to be trustworthy and competent. But this person does not have to be perfect. Many people never sign their wills simply because they can't find the perfect person to be their executor. To avoid stalling on this point, I advised my clients to consider four logical possibilities, and select the best one for their circumstances.

The four possibilities, which are discussed in more detail later in this chapter, include:

- An individual (e.g., friend or family member)
- A professional (e.g., lawyer or other professional advisor)
- A trust company
- The Public Trustee of your province

1. Choosing the Right Executor

As I said, your executor's job is to find all your assets, pay all your debts, and distribute what's left to your beneficiaries according to your will.

That sounds easy, but unless you have been an executor you do not know what an executor's job really involves. I spent 20 years practising law and drafted hundreds of wills, but I certainly didn't have a clue what the average executor was up against until I started working as a trust officer for a trust company. Trust companies are routinely named as executors in wills and trust officers do the work. As a result, I discovered what it was like to walk into a stranger's home to look for and protect the assets. That's also when I discovered how long it could take before those assets could be distributed as directed in the will.

So who should be your executor? The best way to answer this question is to ask two more questions, "What does an executor do?" and "Who would be a good executor?"

1.1 What does an executor do?

Here's a list of some of the things the trust company had to do after the death of someone who had named the trust company as executor in his or her will:

- Figure out how to get into the person's house or apartment
- Food had to be sorted into perishables and non-perishables and then disposed of (perishables usually went in the garbage bin while dry goods were donated to the local food bank)
- The refrigerator and freezer had to be emptied, cleaned, turned off, and left open to air out
- Cleaning supplies had to be sorted and removed
- Pots and pans, linens, bathroom supplies, boxes in the basement, clothes, books, tools, lawn mowers, cars, and many other items had to be dealt with
- Every dresser drawer, housecoat pocket, old envelope, cardboard box, and kitchen cupboard had to be searched through to prevent important papers, savings bonds, jewellery, stock certificates, or a $1,000 bill from inadvertently going out with the trash

Have you noticed that we haven't begun talking about the part that most people are interested in, which is handing out the money and assets to the beneficiaries? Bills and debts have to be found and paid before the money and assets can be released to the beneficiaries. These run from the obvious expenses (i.e., the last phone, cable, heat, light, and water bills) to the less obvious expenses (i.e., credit card bills, loans, and debts). You must remember that the funeral and burial expenses also need to be paid. Above all, don't forget that Canada Revenue Agency (CRA) is the biggest and most powerful creditor of all and it will need its share.

Old tax returns, incidentally, are an excellent source of information for executors. They will tell you a lot about the deceased's financial assets. Also, if the deceased kept good records, finding and paying debts is easy, but many people are not very organized, and some don't file tax returns at all. Then the executor becomes a detective who has to hunt down that kind of information as best he or she can.

Finally, the day comes when the executor is ready to distribute the deceased's property, but what if he or she can't find the beneficiaries? The executor could be holding on to the deceased's assets for a long time while that gets sorted. If all this seems like a lot of work for a trained professional such as a trust officer, what about the normal person who has never done anything like this before? The executor has to squeeze it all into his or her normal day — between getting the children to school and going to work. Being an executor is a big job, so how do you know you are picking the right person for it?

1.2 Who would be a good executor?

Being an executor is a big job that takes time. In fact the law gives the executor one year from date of death, referred to as the *executor's year*, to get the average estate done. Here is a list of some of the more common things that your executor must take care of during that first year:

- Look after funeral arrangements
- Notify necessary people and institutions of your death
- Find your will
- Make sure it is your last will
- Find all your assets
- Make an inventory of your assets

- Determine value of your assets at date of death
- Determine purchase price (adjusted cost base) for capital gains purposes
- Take control of your assets
- Insure and protect your assets
- Apply for pensions, insurance proceeds, and government benefits payable to your estate
- Prepare probate application
- Establish estate bank account
- Sell assets as required
- Advertise for creditors
- Pay your debts
- File any necessary tax returns
- Pay taxes
- Obtain a tax clearance certificate
- Locate beneficiaries
- Distribute assets as your will requires
- Set up and fund any trusts in your will
- Prepare estate accounts
- Distribute accounts as required
- Prepare releases for beneficiaries
- Send releases to beneficiaries
- Distribute assets after releases come in
- Pass accounts with the Surrogate Court, if required

That's quite a list, and the truth is it is a simplified list as there are many more categories and subcategories of tasks I could add. The basic point is that your executor needs to know what he or she is doing.

1.3   Is it a gift, a trust, or a life estate?

There are only two ways to give assets to beneficiaries in a will and your executor must understand the difference:

- Make a gift: your executor must give the asset to the beneficiaries as soon as legally possible after your death

- Put it in trust: your executor must hold the assets in trust and care for them responsibly until he or she is able to distribute them to the beneficiaries as required by your will

When your instructions are to *make a gift*, you have created an *immediately distributable estate*, often called an ID estate. When your instructions are to *set assets aside in trust* and hold them until a future event, you have created a *trust estate*.

Of course, both may be found in one will: you can tell your executor to pay some beneficiaries as soon as possible, and to hold the rest for other beneficiaries in trust. This is done when some of the beneficiaries are incapable of handling the money on their own for various reasons (e.g., the beneficiaries might be too young or seriously disabled).

Actually, there is a third way to transfer assets in your will. You can give them to beneficiaries for their use and enjoyment during their lifetime, with a proviso that when they die, the asset goes to someone else. This is called a *life estate*, which has been used by people who ultimately wanted their estate to go to their children, but they wanted their spouse to have the use and enjoyment of the assets for the balance of the spouse's lifetime. The life estate is not very common today for two reasons:

- Most couples own their major asset (their home) jointly with right of survivorship.

- A trust can be used to accomplish the same end with specific clauses to reflect the needs of each situation.

To better understand the role of the executor, let's look at the example of a young married couple who have only probate-free assets.

If one of them dies, the transfer of joint assets with right of survivorship is automatic. The executor must still attend to all the items listed earlier. Since the will would handle only assets in the deceased's sole name and since the couple know all about each other's assets, there shouldn't be any surprises. Who would they pick as executor of their wills? The obvious choice is each other, which is what the majority of couples do.

The problem gets much more complicated, however, when the survivor dies. Then, there usually aren't any probate free assets because everything was transferred to the survivor when the other died. That means everything must pass under the survivor's will.

Let's assume there are young children and the will says that everything is to be held in trust until the children reach age 21. Already a new problem has arisen: the executor must set up and fund the trust for the children. The executor is now taking on a whole new set of responsibilities (those of a trustee) that will go on as long as there is money in the trust.

Some wills appoint a separate person, a trust company, or a combination of the two as trustees for the children, especially if the estate is large and the money has to be managed for a long time.

The following list includes some of a trustee's responsibilities:

- Invest the estate prudently within the limits prescribed by the Trustee Act of the province, or in harmony with special investment instructions in the will

- Monitor the trust investments carefully, keep accurate records, and be prepared to report to the authorities, or the family as required

- Make reasonable payments from time to time for the upkeep of the children, if the will so states

- File tax returns annually for the trust because trusts are taxable entities in Canada

- Become intimately familiar with the clauses of the will regarding investments and the trust

- Know when he or she can and cannot hire help and determine a reasonable fee to pay for it

- Understand basic principles of trust law such as not delegating decision making to others, maintaining an even hand among beneficiaries, and avoiding a conflict of interest with the trust and the beneficiaries

In other words, the executor's job gets much more complicated if there is a trust to look after, and these trustee responsibilities may last for a long time.

1.4 What powers should I give my executor?

A will prepared by a lawyer usually has a set of powers in it that are designed to make the executor's task easier. These powers are like a toolbox that contains everything the executor might need to do the job after you die. If the executor does not need them there is no harm done; they are just ignored. But if he or she does need them, they are very useful. I have included my own set of powers in both the basic and advanced wills on the CD. So you will understand the purpose of each power, I have listed the powers in the Resources section in the chapter "Executor's Powers" with a heading and a brief explanation about each one of the following:

- Exercise of property rights
- Realization and sale
- Payments to beneficiary
- Distribution in kind
- Investments
- Tax elections
- Employment of agents
- Apportionment of receipts
- Encroachment of power
- Borrowing
- Real property
- Corporate and business assets
- Renewal of guarantees
- Resolution of disputes

Powers are optional and we don't know which, if any, your executor might need when you die. You could select only the ones that you think will apply to your estate, but it is just as easy to put in the whole list. If your executor doesn't need all the powers listed, there is no harm done, but if your executor needs one and it is not there, he or she will have to get a court order to proceed.

1.5 An individual as executor

Most people give the job of executor to a family member or friend. That makes sense when the will sets up immediate gifts of property with no ongoing trusts. However, if there are assets that must be probated or that must be held in trust for a long period, a friend or family member may not be the best choice.

1

Ask yourself the following questions:

- Is your friend or relative capable of handling all the responsibilities?

- Is this person comfortable with this kind of work?

- Has he or she been involved in something like this before?

- Will this person have time to deal with all the duties of being an executor?

- Does he or she know how to keep track of everything and prepare financial statements?

- Has this person had experience working with lawyers, accountants, and financial institutions?

- Is this person prepared to file the necessary tax returns?

- Can the individual do this at a time of grief and loss?

Note: An individual executor is not condemned to suffer through this alone. The law allows an executor to hire an agent to assist him or her with some or all of these tasks, and most individual executors do that, especially if he or she needs to probate the will. For example, the lawyer doing the probate will usually provide additional services to the executor — as agent of the executor — for a fee.

I think it is only polite to ask someone if they will be your executor before you say so in your will. Most people will say yes, but they appreciate being asked ahead of time. Also, note that the appointment of an executor in your will is not binding. You can change your executor any time by changing your will and the executor can refuse the appointment after you die. That's why you need a backup executor in your will, called an alternate, so he or she can step in if the main executor declines to act. (There is more information on alternate executors in section 3.)

1.6 A professional person as executor

Many people ask a lawyer or another professional advisor whom they respect and trust, to be their executor. Some professionals are willing to do so, others aren't. Be sure to ask first, but don't be surprised if the answer is "no thanks." Here is a list of some of the questions that professional advisors ask themselves before agreeing to be an executor:

- How will I charge for this?

- Are there any family conflicts that might make this task difficult?

- Am I insured for this?

- Am I still performing my normal professional services, at my normal rates, for this family?

- Do I have the time to do this and my normal work too?

- Do I know enough about executor's responsibilities?

- Is this going to be like the last estate, which took a lot of time away from my normal work?

The question of fees will never be very far from the surface of a professional's mind, not because he or she is a mercenary, but because they know that being an executor is a lot of work, which could easily interfere with the operation of his or her normal business.

When it gets right down to it, don't be surprised if a professional refuses to be your executor. After all, if he or she wanted to be a professional estate administrator that person would have gone into that business in the first place. Professional advisors usually prefer to assist your executor when the time comes by providing the services they specialize in.

The one exception to this is lawyers. Because lawyers work with wills and estates, many of them are willing to be appointed as an executor for their clients. However, the same questions come up, especially the one about fees. A recent Alberta case made it clear that a lawyer acting as executor is not automatically allowed to charge for executor's work on the suggested executor's fee guideline the way an ordinary executor could. The judge recalculated the lawyer's bill on the basis of what was done and how much it was worth, which turned out to be substantially less than the guideline figure.

The only way around this is if the lawyer sets his or her executor's fees in advance and it is fixed in the will itself. I never did that, and never saw it done by other lawyers, but it is the preferred method of the next group of potential executors — trust companies.

1.7 A trust company as executor

1.7a A corporate executor: Trust companies

Trust companies, or the trust departments of the banks, are still in the business of acting as executors and trustees of private trusts and estates. However, their estate and trust services are not for everyone because of the fees they must charge. Each trust company has a minimum fee for an executor's work so your estate must be more than their minimum value before the trust company will agree to act as executor or trustee. The minimum estate size varies, but as of this writing I suspect that most trust companies won't get involved unless the estate has at least 1 million dollars in gross assets.

Note: Even though trust companies are in business to make money, they can't escape the limits on executor's fees mentioned earlier. To stay onside with those restrictions, the trust companies have standard fee agreements that they will ask you to sign when you appoint one executor of your will and the fees in the agreements run to the high end of the provincial scales. Also, the trust company will make sure that the signed fee agreement is specifically referred to in your will and in all provinces except Manitoba these fee agreements cannot be challenged in court.

A trust company can be a good choice as executor when —

- Your estate consists of at least $1,000,000 gross assets. (Some trust companies may accept smaller estates; you have to ask.)

- You know that a family feud will break out after you die and you want an experienced neutral party to manage your estate until the dust settles.

- Your estate includes complex assets that require sophisticated management or lead to challenging tax problems (e.g., land, a business, publicly traded shares, art collections).

- You have no one to appoint as executor (e.g., no spouse, children, friends, or professional advisors who are ready, willing, and able to do the job).

- You are comfortable with the trust company's fees.

The advantages of a trust company are that they offer a high level of skill and experience for a fixed fee, and the trust company you choose will probably still be in business when you die. The big disadvantage is that their fees only make sense for larger estates.

1.7b Trust companies as agents for executors and trustees

As mentioned earlier, even if you do not choose a trust company as executor, your executor could hire one as an agent to assist with your estate after your death.

Note: The law does not allow an executor to delegate his or her decision-making authority to an agent. However, an executor can decide what needs to be done and hire an agent to do it. For example, an executor may not have the time for the typical tasks such as sorting through the deceased's personal belongings, finding all the assets, insuring the assets, arranging for a lawyer to get probate of the will, contacting the beneficiaries, and preparing tax returns. The executor might be grateful for the assistance of an experienced trust officer who can explain everything, advise him or her on decisions, and then carry out instructions (for a fee of course). Most trust companies have executor assistance services that they actively promote.

1.7c The Public Trustee

The final option, often referred to as the executor of last resort, is the government official in your province called the Public Trustee. The usual responsibility of the Public Trustee is looking after the estates of people who don't have anyone to do it for them including the indigent, the incapacitated, and minors. However, if appointed in a will, they usually accept the appointment if there is no one else available and willing to do the job.

That does not mean that the Public Trustee only looks after small estates. In fact, the Public Trustee is often appointed executor of large estates when there is a court battle involving the handling of the assets or the interpretation of the will.

Like trust companies, the Public Trustee charges a fee for its work. Consult your Public Trustees office for the exact amount before choosing it as the executor of your will. (A list of contact information is included on the CD in the file Contact Info for Public Trustees.)

2. Joint Executors

You can name more than one executor in your will, but if you do, be aware that they must act unanimously. For example, if one executor is opposed to the sale of an estate asset for some reason, the sale cannot proceed. If they can't work it out, the only way around the deadlock is for the other executors to apply to the probate judge for an order approving the sale. That takes time and costs money and most people want to avoid that.

If you do insist on more than one executor, you can avoid the possibility of a deadlock by specifying in your executor clause that the majority rules.

3. Alternate Executors

You should have one or more backup executors — called "alternates" — who can take over if one or more of your executors are unable to do the job. If not, someone will have to make a court application to have a replacement executor appointed.

4. Payment to Your Executor

You will also note that both the Basic and Advanced Will Forms on the CD include the following clause:

> *My Trustees may pay themselves a reasonable fee for the work they do, in addition to any gift or benefit that I leave them in this Will, provided that the amounts are either —*
>
>   *a. approved by the Surrogate Court, or*
>
>   *b. approved by all of the beneficiaries of my estate.*

This covers the common situation in which you appoint someone executor who is also getting something as a beneficiary in your will. There is an ancient law that says that the executor cannot charge a fee for his or her services; he or she can only take the gift in the will. This clause relaxes that rule and allows the executor to charge a fair fee for the work he or she does.

5. Executor Clauses

Review the executor clauses — Step 1: Choose Your Executor Clauses on the CD — and select the one that is appropriate for your will. Note that all clauses refer to the executor and trustee of the will as "My Trustees." This wording stresses the fact that every executor is a trustee of your estate from the time you die until the time they are ready to hand out your property to your beneficiaries. This is true even if you did not create any express trusts in your will requiring your executor to hold property for a long period of time, such as a trust for grandchildren.

Categorize Your Property

Depending on how you own your property when you die, some of your property may not be distributed by your will. That's because some property passes to beneficiaries automatically and other assets can only pass to the beneficiaries after your will has been probated.

This is an important difference, and you need to understand which assets are which when you write your will because assets that pass automatically are not considered to be part of your estate when you die, and therefore they are not affected by what you say in your will. Lawyers say these assets pass outside the will and refer to them as *non-estate assets* or *probate-free assets*. The assets that do pass through your will are called *estate assets*.

1. Non-Estate Assets That Pass Automatically to Beneficiaries

There are two kinds of non-estate assets that pass automatically to beneficiaries outside your will. They are *joint with right of survivorship assets* and *designated beneficiary assets*.

1.1 Joint with right of survivorship assets

Joint with right of survivorship assets are assets that are owned by one or more people jointly, such that when one person dies, his or her share passes automatically to the other joint owner(s). The legal principle that causes this to happen is the *right of survivorship*.

For example, if John and Mary own their house as joint owners with right of survivorship (also called *joint tenancy*) and John dies, Mary takes John's share automatically regardless of what John's will says. However, if John and Mary own their house as joint owners without right of survivorship (also called *tenancy in common*) when John dies, his share goes to his beneficiaries in his will and not automatically to Mary.

It isn't only couples who choose to own assets jointly. An aging parent may decide to put a child on a bank account or even on the title to the parent's home. If so, the same result occurs. If the child is given joint ownership with right of survivorship, then, when the parent dies, ownership of the entire asset automatically goes to the child.

1.2 Designated beneficiary assets

Designated beneficiary assets are Registered Retirement Savings Plans (RRSPs), Registered Retirement Income Funds (RRIFs), Locked In Retirement Accounts (LIRAs), employer pensions, and life insurance policies. Money payable under these plans can automatically pass to a beneficiary at your death regardless of what you may say in your will, if you properly designate the person to receive it when you die. You do that simply by completing the relevant section of the application form when you buy the asset or by filling in a beneficiary designation form.

2. Estate Assets That Pass through Your Will

There are two types of estate assets, those in your name only and those you own jointly with someone else as tenants in common.

2.1 Assets in your name only

If the asset is not a designated beneficiary asset, or if you do not own it jointly with someone else who has right of survivorship, then it is an estate asset and it passes through your will.

2.2   Assets you own as tenants in common

Assets you own as tenants in common are assets that you own jointly with someone else but that person does not have the right of survivorship mentioned earlier so your share of the asset is part of your estate and passes through your will.

Both types of estate assets only pass to the beneficiaries listed in your will and before that can happen your will may have to be probated by a judge of the surrogate court. It is important to realize that your property may consist of both *probate-free assets* and *probate assets*.

Probate-free assets are assets that pass to beneficiaries automatically (i.e., joint with right of survivorship and designated beneficiary assets). Probate assets are assets that only pass through your will and often require probate (i.e., assets in your name only and your share of tenancy in common assets).

Complete Step 2: Categorize Your Property, included on the CD, to identify and classify your property as estate and non-estate assets, keeping in mind that your will only affects your estate assets.

Distribute Your Property

There is no end to the ideas people have for giving property to beneficiaries in their wills. On the CD there are a variety of sample clauses for two common situations: people with children and people without children. These clauses are found in the folder Step 3: Distribute Your Property Clauses. You will also find on the CD Sample 1: Will with Alternate Distribution Clause, which includes information in the margins explaining some of the clauses in more detail.

In my experience people made fairly predictable choices in their wills depending on whether or not they had children. Here is a brief review of the issues they grappled with as they decided what to do with their estate assets in their wills.

1. People with Children

People with children who are living together as a family usually want very specific things to happen when they die:

If one partner dies, he or she wants his or her probate assets to go to the partner so that partner can keep the family together and continue to raise the children after the testator is dead. He or she usually does not give the children any assets until the surviving partner dies.

If both partners die before the children are mature enough to handle large sums of money, they want the children's assets to be held in trust by a dependable trustee who is instructed to divide the probate assets among the children, to invest the money properly, and to pay out reasonable sums for each child's needs before the child reaches a designated age. As each child reaches the designated age, the trustee is instructed to pay the child the balance remaining in that child's account.

If a child does not live to the designated age and has no children of his or her own, his or her share is divided among his or her siblings but if that deceased child leaves any children, the children split his or her share.

If both partners die without any children or grandchildren, they often decide to divide their assets equally among their brothers and sisters, or perhaps leave some to a charity.

To accommodate these possibilities, you need a multi-generational distribution clause that provides for a split of property to the next generation if someone dies before the testator.

Before you can decide who will get your property in your will you must understand the following important legal issues that can have an impact on your distribution decision:

- Can your spouse or children challenge your will if you do not leave them something in it?

- Who should be guardian and trustee of your minor children?

- What happens to your will if you remarry?

Answers to these and other important questions are found in the Resources section of this book in the chapter Frequently Asked Questions. For example, the first question, "Can your spouse or children challenge your will if you do not leave them something in it?" raises the issue of dependant relief laws, which is answered in sections 1.1 and 1.3 in the chapter Frequently Asked Questions.

Note: People with children who are not living together struggle with the same issues though they are usually focused on trying to make sure their ex-partner doesn't get anything in the will. They should get specific legal advice on whether or not the dependant relief laws in their province or territory, or any other laws, apply to them and limit their testamentary freedom before making a will.

2. People without Children

People without children, whether couples or singles, struggle to decide who should get their property. If they are a couple, they usually give their assets to their partner but that doesn't solve the problem of what will happen if the partner dies before they do.

Single people who do not have a partner, of course, face that problem immediately. Where should his or her property go when he or she dies? No one has a natural claim to his or her assets. Consequently, singles without a partner often leave their property to their brothers and sisters. Some people give it to a favourite charity and other people share it with friends.

A single person with children who is divorced or widowed does not have to worry about a spouse making a claim under the family relief law of his or her province. He or she can leave everything directly to the children. If the single person is still married, however, the spouse will have family relief rights, which must be taken into consideration.

Now review the clauses in Step 3: Distribute Your Property Clauses (the "samples" folder on the CD) and select the one that is right for you.

3

Plus One: Sign, Witness, and Store Your Will

1. Sign and Witness Your Will

Signing a will is very simple but if done improperly your will could be invalid. After all the effort you've made so far to get your will done, please don't ruin things by making a mistake now!

Here are the steps to follow:

1. Arrange for two independent witnesses to be with you.

   Independent means the witnesses cannot be —

   • your spouse whether you are a married opposite-sex couple, a common-law opposite-sex couple, a married same-sex couple, or an unmarried same-sex couple, or

   • a beneficiary in your will.

2. Tell the witnesses you are going to sign your will. The witnesses do not have to read your will they just have to know it is your will.

3. Insert the date in the space provided and sign your normal signature in the appropriate space on the last page of the will. Do this only if both witnesses are in front of you and are watching you sign.

4. Put your initials on the bottom right hand corner of all the pages of your will except the last page, which will have your signature.

Initialing the pages is a precaution against someone slipping in a page that doesn't belong in your will at a later date.

5. Ask each witness to sign his or her full name in the appropriate space on the last page of your will. Make sure that you and the other witness watch as each person signs his or her name.

6. Finally, ask each witness to put his or her initials beside yours on all the pages of your will except the last page, which will have your signature and the witnesses' signatures. Again, make sure both witnesses are present and that they watch each other do this.

2. Store Your Will

One of the most common questions that the people at Self-Counsel Press receive from readers is, "Where should I put my will after I've signed it?" If your will was prepared by a lawyer, this isn't a problem because lawyers are happy to store their clients' wills. But when you make a will yourself you don't have that option.

Some people think the probate court or a government office should store it for them because a will is an important legal document. Unfortunately, that is a service they do not provide, so you are on your own.

A common solution is to put your signed will in a safety deposit box at your bank. Let your executor know where it is, and arrange for him or her to have access, if necessary. You don't have to give your executor signing authority to enter your box while you are alive, but you should show him or her where you keep the key. Most banks will let an executor with a key into the box after a death to make a list of the contents and to remove the original will. Then the bank locks the box and doesn't let the executor or anyone else reopen it until the executor returns with a probate certificate from the surrogate court.

Some people do not want to pay for a safety deposit box, so they come up with ingenious ideas for storing their wills. One of my neighbours keeps hers in a plastic bag in her freezer. She says that if the house burns down, the will is surely safe in there, though I wonder what would happen to the ink if the freezer suddenly melted.

Trust companies also store their clients' wills in their own secure storage vaults. If you are naming a trust company as your executor you are entitled to this service at no charge.

In any event, make sure your will is safe from damage and loss, and that it will be easily accessible when needed by your executor.

Resources

Frequently Asked Questions

This chapter covers some frequently asked questions relating to specific content within a will. As well as answering the questions, I have provided some sample clauses that you may consider including in your will. You may also want to refer to Sample 1: Will with Alternate Distribution Clause on the CD.

1. Questions about Content

1.1 Do I have to give something to my spouse?

This is either a dumb question or a front-burner issue, depending on how your marriage is. Every married client I met took it for granted that the deep bonds of matrimony gave his or her spouse a basic right to all, or at least a significant part of, the estate in the will. But every divorced client for whom the bonds of love had become chains of bondage had absolutely no intention of leaving anything to that very same spouse.

The law begins by giving every will maker the right to testamentary freedom. That means you can do whatever you like in your will. But then another law (often called the Dependants' Relief Act — see Table 1 for the name of the law in your province or territory) whittles that down by giving protection to people who are financially dependent on the will maker — the spouse and children. Details of these laws differ in each province and territory, but the general idea is that a will maker must provide for his or her spouse and their children. If not, the spouse and children can apply to a court judge to get the will changed so that they receive a fair share.

Table 1
DEPENDANT RELIEF LAWS

Province/Territory	Name of law
Alberta	Family Relief Act
British Columbia	Wills Variation Act
Manitoba	Dependants Relief Act
New Brunswick	Provisions for Dependants Act
Newfoundland	Family Relief Act
Northwest Territories	Dependants Relief Act
Nova Scotia	Testators' Family Maintenance Act
Nunavut	Dependants Relief Act
Ontario	Succession Law Reform Act
Prince Edward Island	Dependants of a Deceased Person Relief Act
Saskatchewan	Dependants' Relief Act
Yukon	Dependants Relief Act

If you were to leave your spouse out of your will, you might write something like this:

> *Because my spouse is financially self-sufficient (or because I have already made adequate or generous provision for my spouse during my lifetime), I am not leaving anything further to him/her in my will.*

Matrimonial property laws deal with the consequences of divorce by dividing the property of divorcing spouses. Note that even though divorce ends a marriage, it doesn't cancel a will (see section 1.7 for more information). That's up to the will maker, and a divorce settlement prepared by lawyers usually says that each person gives up any claims to the will or estate of the other. It may also make any arrangements to continue child support if the person paying it dies before the children reach the age of financial independence.

What about opposite-sex couples living common law? What about same-sex couples who are married, as the law of Canada now permits? Finally what about unmarried same-sex couples? What rights do they have? Thanks to recent changes on the law, they all have rights to their deceased partner's assets under the dependants' relief laws. However, this area is technical so you should consult a good estate lawyer for specific legal advice.

1.2 Do I need a will if everything is jointly owned with my partner?

This is a very common (and usually good) reason for not doing a will, especially for married folks, but also for single people who jointly own assets with right of survivorship with a partner or friend. If everything you own is in the right kind of joint ownership, and if only one owner dies, then everything will automatically go to the survivor. But there are three very important conditions here. Joint ownership only works as a substitute for a will under certain circumstances.

1.2a It must be the right kind of joint ownership

There are two very different kinds of joint ownership, and the difference is critical when one of the joint owners dies. If you own everything with your partner in joint ownership with right of survivorship, then your assets will be transferred to your partner upon your death, and an estate plan is not necessary.

1.2b One partner dies before the other

Common sense tells us that it is unusual for two people to die at the same time. In the ordinary course of events, couples and non-married joint owners live to a ripe old age together. But eventually, inevitably, one of them dies, leaving the other alone. You probably know many widows or widowers for whom a will wasn't an issue because everything was jointly owned with right of survivorship, and therefore ownership automatically passed to the survivor.

But we all know that the unlikely can happen. Both partners can die together under not-too-unusual circumstances. Let's say they fly to a sun spot for a holiday, having left the children with Aunt Mary, and the plane goes down. They owned everything together, and didn't do a will. Now what?

1.2c The other joint owner must also be the intended beneficiary at death

Things get even more complicated when the joint ownership is between two people, but one does not intend for the other to get whole ownership of the asset at death, such as an aging parent and one of many children. Let's say Dad dies and Mom decides to put one of the children on her bank account so the child can have access to the money if Mom should ever be unable to look after the banking herself.

The two of them go to the bank and they sign a little card with lots of fine print on the back that they never read, and the bank puts the child's name on the account. It's a simple way of making sure Mom will be looked after, and it is very common. But from a legal point of view, an important change of ownership has just occurred, and, in the wrong hands, that can lead to serious problems.

The fine print on the back of the card almost always says that the account is now "Joint with Right of Survivorship." Sometimes the acronyms "JWROS" or "JROS" are used. When Mom dies, the law presumes that the survivor takes all, which very often is not what Mom intended. She may have wanted all the children to share that money equally, and she may even have put that in her will. But if the joint child exercises his or her right of survivorship over that account, none of the other children will get a penny of it.

And there is another risk. Before Mom dies, the joint child can take money out at any time without Mom's permission or knowledge. If the child is dishonest, or decides that Mom really intended to pay him or her for all the extra work he or she is doing looking after Mom while the brothers and sisters go about their busy lives, there may not be much left to share with the others when Mom dies.

So these joint accounts can present legal problems based on the transfer of ownership that takes place as soon as the card is signed.

1.3 Do I have to leave something to my children?

As mentioned in 1.1 above, dependant relief laws give children the right to support and protection. So even though we all have testamentary freedom, it is restricted as far as children go. However, if your children are financially independent, or are past the age of financial support, then you are free to leave them out of your will if you wish. The age of financial independence and other details vary in each province and territory, so ensure that you get good, local legal advice if this is an issue.

People who are planning to leave someone out of their will always ask if it is a good idea to explain why they are doing that right in the will itself. There are two ways of looking at this. Sometimes the explanation is welcomed and graciously accepted and is a good idea, but sometimes it just fans the flames of anger and disappointment and is a bad idea. I always ask people to think about how they would react if they were on the receiving end of one of these explanations, and then proceed accordingly. Of course, if the person you wish to leave out has a proper legal claim to some of your estate anyway (under the dependant relief laws, for example), it doesn't matter if you explain your decision or not, they can still make that claim.

To leave your children out of your will, you could write:

> Because my children are all older than the age of majority and are self-supporting and do not suffer from any mental or physical handicaps that make it impossible for any of them to earn a living, or because I have already made adequate or generous provision for them during my lifetime, I am not leaving them anything further in this will.

1.4　Who will look after my minor children?

You can name someone in your will to be guardian of your children if you die before they reach the age of majority in your province or territory, but your choice is not absolutely binding. That's because people change and things happen. For example, assume you pick your brother as guardian of your children. He may be a good guy today, but what if he becomes an abusive alcoholic? If you don't redo your will, do you still want your children to automatically go to him? Therefore, whether your will says so or not, the courts have the right to rule on his suitability when the time comes, and to name someone else guardian to protect your children, if necessary.

Parents usually appoint the same person to be trustee of their children's money as well as their guardian. However, if the estate is very large or if the guardian has no skill or talent for managing money, they may choose someone else to be the trustee. This can be a good thing, because you now have two adults working together for the benefit of the children, each having a different area of responsibility — the trustee is looking after the management and investment of the money, including all the record keeping and paperwork (such as filing tax returns for the trusts), while the guardian is looking after the day-to-day decisions, such as where the children go to school, their health care, and their social lives.

1.5　Who will look after my minor children's money?

Most parents assume that if they both die before their children are capable of handling money, their assets should be set aside to be used to raise their children until they are old enough to look after the money themselves. Non-parents may wish to leave money for the benefit of nephews and nieces, the children of friends, or children in general. All these will makers have the same problem: they need a trust. Setting up a trust in a will raises the same three questions that we looked at for the will itself: "Who should I pick as trustee? Who gets what, when? What tools does the trustee need?"

Picking a trustee isn't any different from picking an executor. Many people assume that the executor and trustee will be the same person. However, that doesn't have to be the case. You are free to pick someone else as trustee if you wish. If so, your executor would take charge of your estate and hand over the amount going into the trust when it is legally available for distribution. Your trustee would take it from there, but exactly what does that involve?

Trust funds are held for a long time and must be properly managed. The money must be wisely invested in line with the intentions and directions of the person who set it up. It must be spent for the benefit of the beneficiaries of the trust without prejudice to those who get what is left over when the trust is closed. It's like walking a tightrope, and trustees must walk it without a slip because the safety net is the trustee's own pocket. Their liability is high, and personal. If they slip (i.e., if they don't invest wisely, if they spend too much, or even too little) and there is a loss, they may have to make it up from their own pockets. Do them a favour: when you make a trust in your will, be as clear as you can.

Specify precisely when the trust begins and ends, who the beneficiaries are, and what happens if one dies before the trust ends. Make sure the money or property that is going into the trust is accurately described. Allow for resignation or replacement of the trustee. Name an alternate who can step in if the main trustee steps out or is unable to carry on. Permit the trustee to charge a fee for his or her services. Say when and how the fees are to be paid; specify the percentage or the formula or other method for calculating fees.

The law in every province and territory now gives fairly wide scope to a trustee for investing the assets you leave in trust. Instead of limiting a trustee's range of choices to a list of government-approved investments, each jurisdiction has now adopted the prudent investor rule. It says that trustees can invest trust assets as they see fit, as long as they act reasonably and prudently. This gives trustees much more scope than previously when they were limited to a government-approved list of investments. If you are not comfortable with this wide investment power, you can set limitations on your trustee's investment power in your will. If you wish to do this, contact a good estate lawyer for assistance.

1.6 What if the whole family dies in a plane crash?

This question contains much of the anxiety about the terrors of technology that characterizes urban myths. Fortunately, entire families don't get "wiped out" very often, but it can happen, and when it does, it is terrible.

If you don't say anything about what happens to your estate in that event, the government default will takes over. Why not use your will-making power to make your own plan? Two common options are splitting the estate between your relatives and your spouse's, or giving it all to a favourite cause or charity.

Unfortunately, the less likely an event is, the more trouble we have planning for it. Many people who make all the other tough will-making decisions stall at this one. Don't let something that has a minimal chance of happening derail all the rest of your good, hard work. If necessary, flip a coin — heads for relatives, tails for the charity — to get past this.

1.7 What if I remarry?

Most couples in the throes of marriage breakdown have plenty to worry about. On a first-things-first basis, they are preoccupied with custody of children, alimony, and other immediate issues, and rightly so. Cancelling the mutual wills they signed in happier times — those wills that leave everything to each other if one dies — isn't at the top of that list.

Most people assume the problem will be solved when they get divorced because they think that divorce cancels a will. Until recently, this was simply not true — divorce had no effect at all on a will made during a marriage. However, five provinces have changed the law, at least as far as the ex-spouse is concerned. In Prince Edward Island, Ontario, Manitoba, Saskatchewan, and British Columbia, divorce automatically cancels any gifts made in your will to your ex-spouse. Further, in those provinces, divorce also cancels the appointment of your ex-spouse as executor of your will. Note, however, that the rest of your will remains valid in those provinces.

In all the other provinces and territories your will remains completely valid after divorce.

Normally, when a divorce is finalized, the will problem is solved when the couple signs a matrimonial property agreement to divide their assets between them. These agreements usually have a clause that cancels any claims each has against the other's estate including claims based on wills made during the marriage. As long as nothing tragic happens before that agreement is signed, there is no problem, but if a spouse dies before it is signed, all of his or her will must be followed including gifts to the spouse. So, whether or not you live in a province that cancels spousal benefits in your will on divorce, the best advice is to cancel your will as soon as you realize your marriage is beyond repair.

However, even if you do cancel your will after marriage breakdown, and even if you do live in Prince Edward Island, Ontario, Manitoba, Saskatchewan, or British Columbia, remember that your spouse still has a claim under the dependants' relief law of your province. That means if you die before the divorce is finalized, he or she still has the right to claim a fair share of your estate. There is nothing you can do about that because the dependants' relief laws say no one can ever give up those rights.

There is one thing that does automatically cancel a will in every province and territory, and that is remarriage. This rule does not usually create problems for young people with few assets and no children who remarry, but for older couples with grown-up children and lots of assets, it can be a time bomb.

To illustrate, let's assume Mom died at age 60. Dad, who never was much of a domestic engineer, is padding around the big old house alone because the children are far away pursuing careers and raising babies. Inevitably, Dad finds a new companion and proposes marriage. The happy couple tell their children.

The news is greeted with forced smiles and muted groans. It is unfair to assume that all the children are interested in is their inheritance, but it is often not very far from the surface and, in my experience, it never gets talked about. What upsets the children is the fear that Dad will now be sharing their family assets with someone who isn't part of the gene pool. The fact that the children don't legally own any of those family assets is not the point — the emotions that these late-in-life second marriages unlock are often ferocious. Successful estate planning in this situation can involve more anger management and prevention than anything else.

It is very important to understand that any marriage, not just a second or subsequent marriage, cancels a will. If you did a will while you were single, make sure you redo it after you get married. If you don't, the original will is invalid and your estate passes according to the government default laws. The only exception is a will made in anticipation of a specific marriage to a specific person. Such a will must say something like this:

> *I am going to be married to Susan Rich and I am making this will in contemplation of that marriage. Therefore, I intend this will to be valid now and after that marriage.*

1.8 What about same-sex couples?

In 2005 the federal government passed the Civil Marriage Act which defines marriage in Canada as a union of two individuals regardless of sex. This law made same-sex marriages legal under the Marriage Act of every province and territory in the country.

The Civil Marriage Act also has an impact on wills made by same-sex partners because, as spouses, they now have rights under provincial dependant relief laws. That means they can legally make a claim on the estate of their spouse who does not make adequate provisions for them in the will.

When making a will, I suggest a partner in a same-sex marriage make it clear that he or she is legally married according to the law of his or her province. For example, when appointing your executor, you could say:

> *I appoint my spouse, Dani, to whom I am legally married under the laws of (name of province or territory) as my executor and trustee. Throughout this will I will refer to Dani as either "my spouse" or "my executor and trustee."*

1.9 Why didn't we have any problems when my uncle didn't leave a will?

If your uncle didn't have a will, all this means is that he chose to leave his assets to his next of kin in the order, and amounts, set out in the will the government wrote for him. In Canada, each province and territory makes its own laws on matters of property and civil rights, which includes wills and estates. Even though the details are different from one province and territory to the next there is a general pattern, which is summarized in Table 2. The list below is the usual order followed:

- Husband or wife
- Children
- Grandchildren
- Great-grandchildren
- Parents
- Brothers or sisters

Table 2
SUMMARY OF INTESTATE SUCCESSION LAWS

If you die without a will and you have:	Your assets will go to:
A spouse only	That spouse
Children but no spouse	Those children equally
A spouse and children	Your spouse (who gets a defined amount) and the remainder is divided among the spouse and children as the provincial law directs. Exceptions: In PEI and Newfoundland, assets are split equally among your spouse and children. In Manitoba, all goes to your spouse.
No spouse or children	Your closest living next of kin starting with your parents; if neither are alive, then your brothers and sisters or their children; if none of them are alive, then any other next of kin; if none of them are alive, then the provincial government.

As always, please consult the law of your province or territory for specific information (see Table 3).

Let's look at some common results of your uncle's decision not to make his own will:

- Your uncle wasn't fussy about choosing an executor to take charge of and distribute his assets, so he left that choice up to the government default will. It has a list of relatives and others who have the right to ask a judge to give them this job.

- He wasn't concerned about setting aside any money for his favourite nephews and nieces. The government will gives it to his brothers and sisters; the nephews and nieces get something only if their parent happened to die before your uncle.

- Your uncle didn't care to pick his own trustee, so, if the nephews and nieces do get something, the government rules say their money is handled by the public trustee until they reach the age of majority.

- He didn't expand the opportunities for investing and spending the nephews' and nieces' money while it is in trust, so the Public Trustee's officials will follow whatever investment and spending rules their government permits.

These are some of the biggest, most common problems that can arise when someone dies without a will. For those of you who really did have such an uncle, and who did not have any problems with his estate, be glad. But that doesn't necessarily mean that your own affairs will be settled as easily. The most important point to remember is that you can eliminate the uncertainty and make your own choices in your will. When you think about it, most people would rather do that than leave everything up to the government to decide after they are gone.

1.10 What if I die in 30 years? Everything will be different.

This is another excellent point — which also overlooks the obvious. How can you be sure you are going to live for another 30 years? Isn't it a good idea to accept the possibility that something unexpected could happen before then? When most people think about it, they admit that this excuse doesn't stand up, because they know it is better to leave their loved ones with a plan — no matter how unlikely it is that they will need it — than no plan at all.

Table 3
NAMES OF INTESTATE SUCCESSION LAWS BY PROVINCE AND TERRITORY

Province/Territory	Name of Act
Alberta	Intestate Succession Act
British Columbia	Estate Administration Act
Manitoba	Intestate Succession Act
New Brunswick	Devolution of Estates Act
Newfoundland	Intestate Succession Act
Northwest Territories	Intestate Succession Act
Nova Scotia	Intestate Succession Act
Nunavut	Intestate Succession Act
Ontario	Succession Law Reform Act
Prince Edward Island	Probate Act
Saskatchewan	Intestate Succession Act
Yukon	Intestate Succession Act

2. Questions about Form

2.1 Can I change my mind?

Of course you can change your mind, as long as you haven't made a binding contract not to. (That kind of contract is so uncommon these days it doesn't deserve mention.) Some couples make mirror wills that reflect each other (i.e., they are the same except the names are different). They are not considered joint wills (which say that they won't be changed without the other's consent) and can be changed individually at any time. The important thing to remember is that making mirror wills does not constitute making such a contract, unless the wills expressly say so.

If you do decide to change your will, there are two options:

- you can do a new will and cancel the old one altogether, or
- you can do an amendment on a separate piece of paper, which lawyers call a codicil.

I always prefer doing a new will because it is so easy to do — thanks to word processing — and I have found that separate pieces of paper are never around when you need them.

2.2 If I do a will now, will it take away my options for later?

This objection comes in two variations:

- many people believe that a will is forever: if they sign a will today, they give up their right to make changes to it tomorrow, and
- some people also believe that making a will sets everything in concrete and that they have to leave all their assets as is for the will to work.

Fortunately, neither is true in the vast majority of cases. If they were, no one would ever do a will. The fact is that after signing a will, you are completely free to tear it up and make a new one at any time. You are also free to buy new assets and sell existing ones.

Now, sometimes you may want a particular item (the family *Bible*, perhaps) or a certain piece of real estate (perhaps the cottage) to be left to a specific person. And if you no longer own those assets when you die, questions arise, such as —

- is the executor supposed to buy a replacement, or does the person get nothing?
- if the deceased gave the asset to the person named in the will before death, does the rest of his or her gift get reduced accordingly?

Rather than leave these thorny issues to be settled after your death, often at great expense to your estate and great heartbreak to your loved ones, you can simply answer them in your will by giving clear directions about what to do if one of these situations occurs.

2.3 "Doing a will means I'm ready to die — and I'm not!"

This is a very common excuse, and not as silly as it may seem. After all, who wants to sit around thinking about what has to happen after they are dead? Most of us have a hard enough time getting a handle on what has to happen while we are alive!

But when you think about it, it is just another excuse. There is no scientific evidence that I am aware of that proves that people who do wills are more likely to die than people who don't. Fear of death is a very real fear for everyone, but it isn't a good excuse for not doing a will.

2.4 What if I'm too busy right now?

So who isn't busy? This must be the secret mantra of contemporary western civilization. Of course we are too busy: modern life is designed to make us all too busy. Ironically, authors are making fortunes from books on how to take the "busyness" out of life, which people faithfully buy, then are too busy to read!

Most of those books talk about the need to prioritize, and to stick to those priorities. If you've read this far in this book then I bet one of your priorities is to make a thoughtful, comprehensive will. You would rather leave your loved ones a solution than a problem. If that is so, then you are prepared to make time in all the "busyness" to get that done, and you will.

2.5 How is a will signed?

A formal will must be signed by the will maker and two independent witnesses who all see each other sign in the same room at the same time. "Independent" means that the witnesses cannot be a spouse of the will maker, nor can they be a person who is a beneficiary in the will. They must all be adults and of sound mind. Remember, unmarried opposite-sex couples living common law and also same-sex couples whether married or not are now considered to have the same or similar rights as opposite-sex spouses, so don't let your partner witness your will under any circumstances. If he or she does, he or she is automatically disqualified from receiving any of the gifts in your will.

Most lawyers also have the will maker and the witnesses initial each page of the will, but this is not necessary for the will to be valid. It does, however, show that all the initialled pages were part of the original will and that nothing was inserted later on.

2.6 Can my family be witnesses?

If you intend to give members of your family something in your will, they cannot witness your will. Any witness who is also a beneficiary in the will is disqualified from receiving anything under that will, whether family or not. This discourages undue influence where someone could pressure you into signing a will in his or her favour. After you die, you won't be around to explain your reasons so, as protection for you, the law doesn't accept it.

2.7 Does a will have to be typed?

A will can be typed, be in handwriting, or it can be a fill-in-the-blanks form such as the wills included on the CD. Whatever form it takes, it must be signed by you at the bottom, in front of two independent witnesses who see you sign and then sign in front of each other. This is referred to as a formal will, but it isn't the form of the document that matters, it's the formality of signing it.

Note that Alberta, Saskatchewan, and Manitoba recognize holograph wills. As long as these wills are completely handwritten by the will maker, they needn't be witnessed. Holograph wills, however, are often incomplete or confusing. For example, there may not be an executor appointed, or there may be money in trust for minors, but no trustee is appointed to hold it, or property may be gifted to one person in one paragraph only to be taken back and given to another in the next. I have seen very simple holograph wills that were acceptable, but there are many, many more that are incomplete. If you have one, and are concerned about its legal validity, I recommend you take it to a good will and estate lawyer for review.

2.8 Can I do a will on videotape?

No. A videotaped will might be an interesting souvenir, but it is not legal and binding anywhere in Canada at this time.

2.9 When should I review my will?

Lawyers are fond of telling clients to review their wills every five years, or seven, or ten, or whatever number they like. This is good advice that meshes neatly with a lawyer's file recall system, but it has little to do with people's natural instincts.

There are certain life events that should automatically trigger the thought that the will should be checked — births, deaths, marriages, divorces, inheritances, lottery wins, new jobs, and big moves. If you can raise a red flag in your head every time one of these events happens and take a look at your will, your will then stays current and continues to reflect your wishes.

2.10 What happens to my debts?

Your debts are part of your estate and they must be paid before your executor distributes any of your assets to the beneficiaries. If that doesn't happen, your creditors can sue your executor and collect their money from him or her personally, even if all your estate is gone. One of the most commonly overlooked debts is the income tax owed for the year of death, and one of the most powerful creditors is the government. If your executor forgets to file a terminal tax return for you, plus any returns required for your estate, the Canada Revenue Agency can quite easily collect it from your executor.

An important part of the executor's job, then, is to find all your debts and settle them. He or she does this by going through all your papers looking for unpaid bills. Your executor can also publish a notice to creditors in the local newspaper. If this is properly done, and if a creditor fails to respond within the stated time, the creditor loses the right to collect its debt.

2.11 What if I move?

All provinces recognize wills signed in other provinces. If you move to another province, you should always have your will checked by a local lawyer to make sure it is in accordance with laws such as the ones dealing with dependants' relief. Also, you might want to rethink your choice of executor, trustee, or guardian, and replace him or her with someone who lives closer to your new home.

2.12 What if I want to donate my organs?

The best way to do this is to sign a declaration under your province's organ donation law and carry it in your wallet. That way, your donation can be immediately identified and acted on in the case of a fatal accident. Otherwise, if you simply write it in your will, you take the risk that your gift may not be discovered until after you are buried or cremated. Many families deal with a funeral before they open the will.

2.13 How do I give a specific bequest?

You make a specific bequest in your will by saying that a certain item or a certain amount of money (a fixed-dollar amount or a definite percentage of your estate) goes to a specific person. This is easy to do, but problems can arise if things change after you sign the will. If you no longer own the item at your death, your executor has to know whether you want him or her to buy a replacement to give to the beneficiary, or if you just want the gift to lapse. As for money, if you don't have enough to satisfy the gift when you die, your executor will proportionately reduce the gift unless you say otherwise.

2.14 Burial instructions

It is always a good idea to leave your burial instructions somewhere separate from your will, just in case your friends or family decide to leave the will until after the funeral.

2.15 How can I revoke my will?

You cancel a will by destroying it, by doing a new one that is intended to revoke the old one, or by getting married.

2.16 Can my will be voided?

Your will can be challenged after you die, but only on technical grounds. For example, if your will was not properly signed by you and two independent witnesses in the same room at the same time, it is invalid. Or, if you did not have full mental capacity when you signed it, it is invalid. Also, if you were pressured by someone who made you sign a will that you did not wish to sign, it is invalid if the pressure was truly severe enough to cause you to ignore your own desires and common sense. And, of course, your old will is automatically cancelled when you marry.

3. What Can My Executor Do While I'm Still Alive?

In a word, nothing. Contrary to common opinion, an executor has no power to do anything until you die. Just because you have done a will doesn't mean that there is someone who can manage your financial affairs or make health-care decisions for you if you lose capacity during your lifetime.

That requires two other documents, the Enduring Power of Attorney and the Advance Directive also known as a Living Will. You will find samples of these forms on the CD. For more information see the *Living Wills Kit* and the *Power of Attorney Kit*, both published by Self-Counsel Press.

Executor's Powers

The executor's powers are the typical powers that I included in all my wills. Your executor may not need all of them, but it is better to have a power or two in your will that may not be needed than to not have one that might save your executor and beneficiaries a lot of time and money after you are gone.

1. Exercise of Property Rights

The following clause is intended to enable the executor or trustee to assume all the deceased's property rights, including the right to start or defend any legal actions that may be necessary.

My Trustees may exercise any rights that arise from ownership of any property of my estate. This includes the right to conduct any legal actions necessary with respect to the estate property.

2. Realization and Sale

One of the primary duties of the executor or trustee is to "realize" the estate, which means to convert the assets of the trust into cash and invest the cash in assets that are authorized for by law, or as permitted by the will itself.

The executor or trustee is given an express power of sale so there can be no doubt about the power to sell any part of the estate and to agree to any reasonable terms of sale. The executor or trustee is also authorized to delay a sale if he or she considers it advisable and in the best interests of the beneficiaries. For example, if land or stock values have fallen, it may be better to hold an estate asset for a while and sell when the market improves.

To realize and sell my estate assets on terms my Trustees think advisable. They may delay conversion until it is advantageous. They can hold assets in the form that they are in at my death even if the assets are not approved for Trustees. They will not be responsible for any loss, which may occur from a properly considered decision to leave investments in the form that they were in when I died.

3. Payments to Beneficiary

Technically, only a mentally competent adult can give a legally binding receipt. This rule may restrict your trustee's flexibility in carrying out your wishes. For example, if the trustee wants to make a payment to a minor, or a person who is mentally incompetent, this clause relaxes the technical rule and allows the trustee to accept a receipt from the person's caregiver.

To make any payment for a person younger than the age of majority to his or her parent or guardian and the receipt of that parent or guardian will be a sufficient discharge to my Trustees.

4. Distribution in Kind

This distribution in kind clause allows the executor or trustee to give the beneficiaries assets of equal value rather than cash. For example, if the deceased had three children and he or she owned a boat, car, and snowmobile of approximately equal value, the executor or trustee could give the boat to one child, the car to another child, and the snowmobile to the third child without the cost and delay of selling them.

To transfer the assets of my estate to my beneficiaries without converting them into cash when that is reasonable and for this purpose my Trustees will determine the value of the assets involved and their valuation will be binding.

5. Investments

The law in many provinces restricts a trustee's investment options by pre-scribing a list of authorized trust investments. This clause overrides that law and gives the executor or trustee a broader discretion in making investments. The executor or trustee must still act in the best interests of the beneficiaries, and cannot invest, for example, in speculative stocks or un-secured loans to relatives.

Trustees who act honestly, with ordinary prudence, and within the limits of the trust are not liable for losses that are caused by mere errors of judgment. However, trustees who act negligently may be personally liable for any losses to the estate.

To invest my estate assets in investments that are not authorized for Trustees.

6. Tax Elections

The tax elections clause allows the executor or trustee to arrange for any after death tax planning that might be possible under the tax laws in force when the testator dies.

To make any elections available under the Income Tax Act of Canada or any other applicable statute.

7. Employment of Agents

The clause for employment of agents allows the executor or trustee to use the professional services of a trust company or other estate administration professionals for administrative and accounting matters, but the executor or trustee is the only one who makes decisions and exercises discretion under the will.

To employ any agent to carry out the administration of my estate and its trusts.

8. Apportionment of Receipts

If money is being held in trust and is earning interest or other revenue, the clause for apportionment of receipts gives the executor or trustee the power to designate that revenue as either capital or income in order to minimize tax and simplify administration.

To decide whether receipts are income or capital in his or her discretion.

9. Encroachment Power

When assets are held in trust for a period of time, it is natural to ask whether the property can be used for the benefit of the beneficiaries before they reach the qualifying age and, if so, to what extent. This is called the power of encroachment.

Even if all the will maker's children are adults, the will may still need a power of encroachment for grandchildren or others who may be minors. For example, if your will says that the share of a child who predeceases you is to pass to that child's issue, it is possible the grandchild will be a minor. If there is any chance of a minor becoming a beneficiary under your will, you will have to consider whether your executor or trustee is to be able to encroach for that beneficiary's benefit.

The following example is a broad power of encroachment:

Except as otherwise provided in this Will, if my Trustees hold any share of my estate in trust he or she shall have the power to spend as much of the income or capital or both as my Trustees consider advisable for the maintenance, education, advancement, or benefit of the beneficiary of that trust.

10. Borrowing

The borrowing clause and the three clauses that follow are usually only inserted in the wills of people who have businesses. These clauses give the executor or trustee increased power and flexibility to deal with the business and to wind up the estate's involvement in the business in an orderly way.

To borrow money for the estate with or without security.

11. Real Property

To manage, sell, or lease any real property in my estate on such terms as they choose and to spend such amounts as may be necessary to maintain and repair it.

12. Corporate and Business Assets

a) *To represent my estate as a shareholder in any corporations in which it holds shares and to participate in any corporate decisions required.*

b) *To carry on any business I was engaged in as if I were still alive.*

c) *To incorporate a company to carry on any business or hold any assets of my estate.*

13. Renewal of Guarantees

To renew any Guarantees or Securities I may have given to secure the debt of another person and to renew them only for the purpose of an orderly liquidation. I direct my Trustees to do this without undue embarrassment to my family or business associates.

14. Resolution of Disputes

If any dispute arises over the interpretation or validity of this will, I direct my Trustees to pursue all reasonable ways to resolve it, including mediation and arbitration, before resorting to litigation.

Estate Planning for Life: The Law of Aging

Most people who consider doing their wills have no idea that there are any other estate-planning documents to be concerned with, but there are. They are related to the law of aging. If you are like most people, you probably won't discover this area of law until you start looking after an aging loved one and you reach a point where your informal decision-making authority falls short. Let me tell you about the kind of phone call I often received in my law office.

Note: For convenience, I am using the terms used in Alberta, which may be different from the ones used in your province or territory. However, these situations — and the basic rules of the law of aging — are the same everywhere, simply because people get old and don't always plan for it, no matter where they live. Refer to Tables 4 and 5 at the end of this chapter to find out what terms are used in your province or territory.

An aging widower starts to decline mentally and physically. His daughter gradually takes over more and more of the daily chores, such as banking, bill paying, and grocery shopping. This informal care works and keeps Dad in his own home for several years.

Unfortunately, Dad reaches the point where he is not safe living on his own at home. He is forgetting to turn off the stove-top burners and is locking himself out regularly. His daughter gets Dad to sign cheques but he doesn't really know what account is being paid. His daughter arranges for home care to come in twice a week, but that is not enough, and with government cutbacks, she can't get them to come more frequently. It's time for Dad to go to a nursing home, and that is done.

The house is now empty, so the daughter calls a real estate agent and, even though he is confused, Dad signs a listing agreement. The house is in a stable, central neighbourhood that is popular with young couples.

During a family meeting at the nursing home, a staff member says something about the daughter having to get a substitute decision-making order. The daughter is annoyed. She has been doing everything for years, and nobody ever said anything about a court order before. When she asked for help, the government told her there was no more available. Does the same government mean to tell her that she has to see a lawyer and spend money on some fancy paper just so she can continue doing exactly what she has already been doing and is going to keep on doing no matter what anybody says? The staff member gives her the phone number for the local seniors' society, which keeps track of lawyers who do this work. The daughter says thanks, and does nothing.

A few days later, the real estate agent has an offer for more than the asking price. Dad still isn't sure what this is all about, but he dutifully puts his signature on it. Then the agent wants to know where to send the legal work to close the deal.

The daughter calls the seniors' society, and they give her a list of lawyers to call. She calls me and asks if I do real estate. I ask some quick questions to get the picture and learn about the pots on the stove, the cheque writing procedure, the nursing home move, the empty house, and the proposed sale.

This was a routine call for me, but it was not a routine situation for this daughter. She had never been through anything like this before. Even though the daughter thought she was just calling about a house sale, I suspected it was much more than that. Here are some more questions I would typically ask:

- Is the title to the house in Dad's name alone?

- If Mom is still a joint owner, have steps been taken to remove her from the title?

- Did Dad really understand the offer when the agent explained it?

- Can Dad call me himself?

- Why is he in the nursing home?

- What do the doctors say about his mental capacity?

- Can he get to my office?

- Is he capable of signing all the other legal documents we need?

- If he can't sign, does anyone have legal authority to sign for him?

- If so, where does that signing authority come from?

- If not, do we have enough time to get legal signing authority before closing?

- Who will look after Dad's money after the sale closes?

- Does the insurance company know the house is vacant?

Assuming that the answers are either "No" or "I don't know," I now have very good reason to believe that Dad is no longer capable of managing his affairs, and I can no longer behave as if he is fine. That means that this good daughter is about to collide with the brick wall of the law of aging. She is about to learn about surrogate decision making for the living.

The daughter has done the right thing; she used her informal authority properly and wisely as far as it would go. Many people and institutions happily accepted her say without question, but there are many who won't, or can't. One institution in every province that requires formal legal authority is the land registration office. Their staff aren't in the business of turning over title to somebody's land on the mere say-so of a well-meaning relative or friend. This is a good thing: I don't want my house being sold or mortgaged by my spouse or a family member without my approval any more than you do. If there is doubt about Dad's ability to understand and sign land documents, relatives can't do it unless they can show specific legal authority giving them the right to exert control over Dad's property.

This kind of formal substitute decision-making authority can only come from one of three places. Unfortunately, a loving relationship isn't one of them. The authority can come only from —

- a general law of the province in which Dad resides, establishing automatic rules for substitute decision-making authority,

- an enduring power of attorney, created and signed by Dad, appointing the daughter, or

- a court order giving her specific substitute decision-making authority over Dad.

Only Ontario, PEI, and Saskatchewan have general laws setting up automatic rules. (In Ontario it's the Health Care Consent Act; in PEI it's the Consent to Treatment and Health Care Directives Act; and in Saskatchewan it's the Health Care Directives and Substitute Decision-Makers Act. In all these acts, the person appointed under an advance directive is at the top of the list.) Usually, the daughter must look for a specific document signed by Dad, or she has to get a court order.

The chances of finding an enduring power of attorney are slim, unfortunately. Many people are not aware of them, or if they are, very few have actually done one. Furthermore, the laws allowing for enduring powers of attorney are relatively recent — most were passed in the 1990s. Because of that, and because people who make one usually let the substitute decision maker know about it, the odds of an enduring power of attorney existing without the daughter knowing it are slim. This means she has to head to court for a court order — words that raise vivid, unpleasant images of lawyers, delay, and cost in most people's minds.

I used to tell my clients to allow four to six weeks from the day we had all the medical reports confirming loss of capacity to the day the judge signed the order. The cost was in the neighbourhood of $1,500 if other family members didn't oppose the request. If they did, then we headed into the open-ended process of litigation — another legal word that raises vivid and uncomfortable images in people's minds, for very good reason.

If Dad were still competent and could understand and sign his own enduring power of attorney, then we could do that. But if he isn't, the choice is get the court order or lose the sale, and losing the sale is never a good choice. Insurance companies are nervous about insuring vacant properties for too long, and caregivers usually have enough to do without becoming landlords as well — especially when they don't have legal control over the property they will be renting. We inevitably got the court order, but not without a good deal of anger and frustration.

So we solved the house sale problem. However, the daughter doesn't know it, but the real story is just beginning. This court order makes the daughter a trustee of Dad's assets, and puts some heavy responsibilities on her. These vary from province to province, but in Alberta they include the following:

- She has six months from the date of the order to file a sworn inventory at the court house detailing all Dad's assets and money, not just the house.

- She must file detailed accounts showing what happened to all of Dad's assets — every penny that came in and every penny that went out — and have these accounts reviewed by a judge every two years.

- She cannot pay herself for her effort without court approval.

- She must come back to court to have the order reviewed and continued every six years.

- She does not have power to make personal or health care decisions about the dependent adult (Dad) unless she also asked to be Dad's guardian (a guardian is the person who has authority under a court order to make decisions about health and personal care, while a trustee is appointed under a court order to look after the assets and financial matters).

- She can invest Dad's money only in certain assets, unless otherwise permitted.

Obviously, if the daughter is going to be a trustee of Dad under such a court order, she must have the same skills and knowledge as an executor or trustee under a will. At the very least, she must know how to set up and maintain a good record-keeping system. Otherwise, she, her accountant, or her lawyer will have a box full of two years' worth of paper to sort out at the last minute. That kind of neglect might even lead the reviewing judge to wonder if the daughter was perhaps not the best person for this demanding job in the first place. If the daughter is careless to the point of losing some of Dad's money — or if she uses it for unauthorized purposes — a judge usually has power to dismiss her and appoint someone else. Of course, she would be liable to make up any losses out of her own assets.

This common example amounts to a crash course in the law of aging for the caregiver generation. Faced with a short-fuse crisis around the sale of Dad's house, clients in this situation get the idea the hard way: there is more to competent estate planning than a will. After going over the options, and learning about the demands of the court order, every single one of these clients said, "If only Dad had signed an enduring power of attorney, how much cheaper, faster, and easier this would be." How true. So let's turn back the clock to when Dad was making his will and go over the planning opportunity that he missed — the two remaining estate planning documents he could have done: the enduring power of attorney and the advance directive.

Table 4
ENDURING POWER OF ATTORNEY LAWS AND TERMS BY PROVINCE AND TERRITORY

Province/ Territory	Name of law	Name of document	Name of decision maker
Alberta	Powers of Attorney Act	Enduring Power of Attorney	attorney
British Columbia	Representation Agreement Act	Representation Agreement for Property or Finances	representative
Manitoba	Powers of Attorney Act	Springing Power of Attorney	attorney
New Brunswick	Property Act	Power of Attorney	attorney
Newfoundland	Enduring Powers of Attorney Act	Enduring Power of Attorney	attorney
Northwest Territories	no law		
Nova Scotia	Powers of Attorney Act	Enduring Power of Attorney	attorney
Nunavut	no law		
Ontario	Substitute Decisions Act	Continuing Power of Attorney for Property	attorney for property
Prince Edward Island	Powers of Attorney Act During Legal Incapacity	Power of Attorney	attorney
Saskatchewan	Powers of Attorney Act	Enduring Power of Attorney	attorney
Yukon	no law		

Table 5
ADVANCE DIRECTIVE LAWS AND TERMS BY PROVINCE AND TERRITORY

Province/ Territory	Name of law	Name of document	Name of decision maker
Alberta	Personal Directives Act	Personal Directive	agent
British Columbia	Representation Agreement Act	Representation Agreement for Health Care	representative
Manitoba	Health Care Directive Act	Health Care Directive	proxy
New Brunswick	no law		
Newfoundland	Advance Health Care Directives Act	Advance Health Care Directive	substitute decision maker
Northwest Territories	no law		
Nova Scotia	Medical Consent Act	Authorization to give medical consent	deemed guardian
Nunavut	no law		
Ontario	Substitute Decisions Act	Continuing Power of Attorney for personal care	attorney for personal care
Prince Edward Island	Consent to Treatment and Health Care Directives Act	Health Care Directive	proxy
Saskatchewan	Health Care Directives and Substitute Decision Makers Act	Health Care Directive	proxy
Yukon	no law		

Your Enduring Power of Attorney

1. What Is a Power of Attorney?

The idea of a normal power of attorney has been around for a long time. It is used in situations where you need someone to do something on your behalf. Let's say you are buying a house, but suddenly your company sends you to South America to supervise a six-month project. You could sign a power of attorney appointing your spouse, your lawyer, or anyone else you trust to sign the real estate papers and wrap up the deal for you in your absence. Once the deal is over, or once you get back, the appointment ends and you take control.

Note: In Canada, the term "attorney" means the person appointed in a document, such as a power of attorney, to handle your affairs. It is different from the term "lawyer," which refers to a person with a law degree who is trained to give legal advice. For more information on powers of attorney, take a look at the *Power of Attorney Kit*, another title in the Self-Counsel Press Legal Series.

2. What Is an Enduring Power of Attorney?

People who plan used to think that something similar to a power of attorney made sense in case of the possible loss of their own mental capacity in the future. They wanted to be able to sign a document that would give someone else legal power to take over their financial affairs if they ever became mentally incapacitated. Such a document would be triggered by the loss of capacity.

Unfortunately, the law used to prevent that. It said that normal power of attorney documents were only as good as the person who signed them, so if you became incapacitated, your power of attorney document was automatically terminated. That raised serious doubts about the benefit of using powers of attorney that were triggered by incapacity for estate planning purposes under the law as it stood. If you signed one anyway, and your attorney acted on it, anything your attorney did would be unauthorized and could have serious consequences for him or her.

The only way to fix that was for each province to pass a law specifically permitting powers of attorney for estate planning purposes, and over the past ten years or so they have done just that. Because each province calls this document something different, I will refer to it as the enduring power of attorney to distinguish it from the normal power of attorney discussed above. (See Table 4 in the previous chapter to find out the name used in your province.)

No matter what the provinces call these, there is one thing that all the different enduring powers of attorney have in common — they are very short, often only one page long, covering just the basic points. Typically, these documents —

- Identify the attorney
- Say when the attorney's power begins
- Give the attorney "power to do anything I can do by an attorney."

If you were named attorney under such a document you wouldn't have much to go on, would you? You could fill out more detail by reading your province's Power of Attorney Act, but how many attorneys, most of whom aren't lawyers, have a copy of their provincial act in their pockets?

Many lawyers won't be able to tell you much either, simply because enduring powers of attorney are so recent, and few lawyers have experience being an attorney. Nor do they want it — most lawyers don't want to give up any of their normal fee-generating work to take on the numerous and long-lasting responsibilities of an attorney. However, a large number of enduring powers of attorney written during the past decade are now being triggered. Because many of these documents appoint trust companies as their attorneys, trust officers who have the job of making them work are quickly gaining experience.

Let's look at the issues you should consider when creating your enduring power of attorney. It doesn't matter which province you live in or what the typical document in your province may say; these are general issues that apply to everyone, everywhere.

3. What Are the "Maybes" That an Attorney Must Deal With?

Writing a will is difficult for most of us, but doing an enduring power of attorney is even harder. That's because a will is for death and an enduring power of attorney is for life — our own life. The executor of a will has a big job, but he or she does not have the worry of caring for us while we are still living. The executor's responsibility is to get on with what must be done under the will and hope that he or she has all the power needed to take care of any "maybes" that could arise.

Your attorney, however, doesn't have that luxury. In fact, his or her job is the exact opposite. Your attorney's job, if you become incapacitated, is to protect and manage your estate and to use your assets to look after your financial needs. But the fact that you will still be alive makes the job more complicated. Here are some examples of what your attorney may have to consider:

- You could live for another 6 months or for another 60 years. Your attorney will have to manage your affairs indefinitely and make appropriate decisions.

- You may be able to afford to stay in your home and hire 24-hour care. Perhaps you can afford to buy or rent in a private, full-service seniors' complex. Or, you may have to go to a public nursing home. How will this be decided?

- What does your attorney do if you have dependants who still need financial support?

- Does your attorney keep or sell any rental property you own?

- What if your estate runs short? Does your attorney keep or sell any specific assets you have designated to certain people in your will?

- Can your attorney deal with any specific mutual funds or other investments you have, and sell them if they go bad?

- What if your attorney needs professional help to deal with your affairs? Can he or she get it and pay for it out of your estate?

- Does your enduring power of attorney allow for your attorney to be paid a fair price for his or her work? How much? When?

- Is your attorney able to get into your safety deposit box to get documents?

- What if your attorney has to sell your house? What should he or she do with the contents?

- If your attorney needs to get summaries of your previous tax returns, will he or she have this power?

- If your attorney is not also your health care agent (see the next chapter), how is he or she to work with that caregiver?

The point here is that these issues are unpredictable, which introduces a whole new planning problem for you — "the maybes." Most enduring powers of attorney don't say much about the maybes, for good reason. How much luck have you had predicting the future during your lifetime? Life is capricious; things happen, and we don't always see them coming.

Even so, we owe it to ourselves, and to those around us, to plan. While we cannot anticipate every detail and force it to come true, we can make sure we are standing on a firm foundation and are ready to deal as best we can with whatever life throws our way. In that sense, preparing for the possibility of incapacity means that your enduring power of attorney is the foundation and your attorney is the one who needs to be ready to respond to whatever financial challenges arise as a result of your incapacity.

If you know that certain things will happen — for example, your house will need to be sold — then write them down in your enduring power of attorney with clear instructions telling your attorney what you want him or her to do. The rest you just have to leave in the hands of your attorney, so pick a good one and discuss with your attorney how you feel about the issues listed above so that he or she is aware of and can try to meet your wishes.

Like your will, there are three critical parts to an enduring power of attorney (see Table 6). Each part asks an underlying question that points right to the most important person in the document — your surrogate financial decision maker or your enduring power of attorney.

Table 6
THE LOGICAL STRUCTURE OF AN ENDURING POWER OF ATTORNEY

Part	What It Does	Underlying Question
The setup	Appoints your surrogate financial decision maker (attorney) and backup	Who will be my attorney?
The trigger	Establishes when you have lost capacity and how your attorney knows when to take over	When do I want my attorney to start?
The attorney's toolbox	Gives your attorney power and discretion to handle any potential occurrences related to your affairs (the "maybes")	What does my attorney need in order to do the best job?

4. The Setup, or Who Will Be My Attorney?

Each province has its own technical requirements about who can be an attorney, but, in general, you are free to select any adult person (meaning anyone who has capacity and who your province considers to be of legal age). He or she does not have to live in your province, and there isn't an enduring power of attorney's training course, so no certificates or credentials are required. This gives you very broad scope.

Most people pick a member of their immediate family (i.e., spouse, parent, or child) and leave it at that. But what happens if the spouse becomes an alcoholic or a gambler? What happens if the parent is a good choice but dies, or becomes incapacitated? Just like you did in your will, you can pick a backup attorney, and you should specify when that backup is to step in.

You should look for someone who has all the qualities of a good executor, plus the ability to look after any of the financial maybes that might come your way. The critical difference between an executor and an attorney is that your executor has a rough idea of how long the job should take: the executor's year. But how does your enduring power of attorney know how long he or she will be on the job? Your attorney must be available for the long haul, just in case.

You could choose a relative, friend or neighbour, or a professional person with whom you have a good relationship. Regardless, it must be a person you can trust, because even though you will be there in body, you won't be there in mind to supervise and criticize what he or she does with your hard-earned estate. Many of you are lucky enough to have such a person, and there is no reason not to appoint them if you feel good about it.

If you don't know anyone you feel confident can handle your affairs, you can appoint two or more people and say they have to make all decisions unanimously. If they can't agree, you can set up a tie-breaking mechanism or you can tell them to get a decision from a judge. Remember, though, that the cost involved in going to court would come out of your estate, and the legal work takes time.

Your attorney could be a professional person such as your accountant or lawyer, but chances are they would have the same concerns about being your attorney as they would about being your executor. They would probably also expect to receive a fee similar to their usual professional fees. You should ask them about all this before naming them in your enduring power of attorney.

You can also name a trust company as your attorney. Trust companies prefer to talk to you before you sign your enduring power of attorney so they can tell you about the services they offer, how they prefer to invest your assets, and the fees they will charge. If you decide to appoint one as your attorney, the company likes to talk to the lawyer who is drafting the enduring power of attorney, and it may send him or her sample clauses to insert into the document to make the trust company's job clearer and easier. Your lawyer should review these with you before you sign the document to make sure you understand them and agree to them.

If you can't come to terms with a trust company, then you are sometimes able to appoint the public trustee of your province. Not all public trustees accept enduring power of attorney appointments. In New Brunswick, Alberta, NWT, and Nunavut, for example, they do not. In Ontario they do, but only if you get their written consent before you sign the document. No trustee in the Yukon has ever been appointed, although the territory has no rules against it. The others do, but they always appreciate the chance to talk to you before you sign the document so that they can be sure it complies with their requirements and contains all the powers and provision they need to do the job properly. Check with your local office before you proceed. For contact details of the public trustee in your province, see Contact Info for Public Trustees on the CD.

In case the attorney you name dies or becomes incapacitated and can't do the job, your enduring power of attorney should name a backup attorney. Whomever you choose, your attorney's authority will have to be triggered, as discussed in the next section.

5. The Trigger, or When Do I Want My Attorney to Start?

The executor of your will knows exactly when his or her job starts — when you die. But how will your enduring power of attorney know when to step in? If you are lucky enough to be very close friends with a leading expert on loss of mental function, then you don't have to worry about this, but most of us aren't. How will your spouse, child, partner, best friend, accountant, or trust officer know when you have lost the capacity to make your own decisions? How comfortable will they be having to decide that you can't manage your money and assets anymore and they must take over? Not very. While some people do give this responsibility to the attorney, the enduring power of attorney documents I drafted always did one of the following:

- they designated someone to evaluate competence and trigger the enduring power of attorney, or
- they were effective when signed and were put away until needed.

A specific health care person who knows you, such as your family doctor, home care nurse, psychologist, or social worker, is usually designated to evaluate your competence, but it could be anyone else. The key factor is that it is a person who won't take your money and run while you are still competent.

If you can't think of anyone, or if your family doctor happens to retire and move to Florida before you do, you can designate any two doctors who are familiar with your case.

Either way, the trigger event should be a note in writing, signed and dated by the designated person, and attached to the enduring power of attorney. Otherwise, the outside world won't know if the enduring power of attorney is in effect or not.

The second approach may sound odd, but it works for people who have a long-standing relationship and share a deep-seated trust. It allows them to avoid the poking and prodding that goes along with a medical examination to establish competence. They simply appoint each other and then put the enduring power of attorney in a secure place, such as a safety deposit box, for future use. Both people need to be able to get into the box in an emergency for this to work, of course.

6. The Attorney's Toolbox, or What Does My Attorney Need in Order to Do the Best Job?

This is where you give your attorney powers to handle as many of the potential occurrences related to your affairs (i.e., the "maybes") as you can. This could include power to —

- Manage your personal financial affairs
- Manage and invest your assets,
- Keep or invest your wealth in assets that may not be approved for trustees
- Deal with your real estate
- Pay for your maintenance and benefit
- Obtain professional assistance with managing your assets
- Continue making charitable donations and other gifts on your behalf

- Obtain originals of your important documents
- Dispose of your personal or household items
- Work with your health care agent to pay for the best possible care for you
- Pay himself or herself for his or her services as your attorney as and when you permit

Report to your family or friends as you require

- Keep proper records of his or her handling of your estate

Sample 2: Enduring Power of Attorney on the CD gives you the complete wording of each of these powers. There is a blank form included as well.

As you read this list, you see that there are two big challenges for your enduring power of attorney:

- The challenge of long-term asset management
- The challenge of working with your health care agent

7. The Challenge of Long-Term Asset Management

Some of us have enough trouble looking after our own assets, let alone taking over the job of managing someone else's. Term deposits, GICs, Canada Savings Bonds, corporate bonds, mutual funds, rental properties, pork belly futures, the next Bre-X, the latest dot-com stock — the possibilities are endless and often mind-boggling. But at least we are free to do what we want, and if we goof up, we have no one to blame but ourselves.

Unfortunately, an enduring power of attorney doesn't have the same unlimited scope. The law makes it clear that an enduring power of attorney will be held to the same standard as a formal trustee or any other fiduciary (the legal word for someone who is held to a very high standard of honesty and care when looking after the affairs of someone else). That means no Bre-X or dot-coms. But what if you already have such assets in your portfolio when your attorney takes over?

The law of every province sets a standard for fiduciaries like attorneys and trustees. It is called the standard of the reasonable investor or of the reasonable trustee. This allows a fiduciary to keep investments that are in your portfolio when he or she takes over as long as it is reasonable to do so. It also allows your attorney to use his or her judgment when buying assets for you. Make sure you give your attorney the scope he or she needs to deal with your investments in your enduring power of attorney document.

Every enduring power of attorney document should also give the attorney the power to get, and pay for, outside advice, if necessary. You would turn to a professional for help if you needed it, so why can't your attorney?

8. The Challenge of Working with Your Health Care Agent

Your health care agent is the person you appoint to handle your personal care and health care should you become incapacitated. The next chapter deals with the advance directive and health care agent in more detail.

The line between where an enduring power of attorney's power stops and a health care agent's power begins is not an easy one to draw as far as looking after your physical needs goes. Both are trying to make sure you get the best possible care, but each from a different point of view.

Your health care agent decides where you should live and what you should get, while your attorney has to make sure your estate can afford to pay for it. Therefore, it is vital that these two decision makers can work together. Of course, they can be the same person, which at least eliminates some of the potential conflict, but that isn't always the best solution for everyone.

Try to give some thought to how these two people will work together, and don't be afraid to put something about this into your documents. I have yet to see it done, but why can't both documents say that if the attorney and the agent can't resolve their differences over something, then they have to go to a mediator or some other neutral third party to work it out? Don't leave them with no choice but to go to court and use the money from your estate to settle their differences.

Your Advance Directive

When I worked for a trust company, we often had cases where we were appointed enduring power of attorney for an elderly person who had lost his or her spouse and never had any children. I detail one such case, that of an elderly woman, below. Let's call her Maxine.

Maxine had a lot of money but was alone. When Maxine's doctor sent the letter to the trust company saying she couldn't manage her money anymore, that triggered the enduring power of attorney and we took over. Unfortunately, Maxine didn't sign an advance directive when she signed the enduring power of attorney, so no one had legal power to make decisions about her health and personal care.

That didn't matter too much as long as she was living in her own home and was willing to let the home care workers in. Eventually, the time came for Maxine to go to a care facility. Unfortunately, Maxine didn't agree. A niece came forward to try to help and was thinking about getting a guardianship order, but when Maxine ran her off the property, the good-hearted niece changed her mind.

A short while after that, the local constabulary delivered Maxine to a psychiatric institute where she was held under the Mental Health Act as a person who was a danger to herself, and was diagnosed and treated. She was stabilized, and the day came for her release. But where was she to go? Back to her house where the destructive cycle would begin all over again?

As the only people with any kind of legal authority over Maxine, the trust company was called to see if we would approve sending her to a suitable care facility. We explained that we only had authority to manage her money, not to make any decisions about her personal care, including where Maxine was to live. But the calls kept coming. Finally I said that while we couldn't approve placement in any particular facility, we did have power to pay the bills once a suitable facility was found and she was placed, as long as the bills were reasonable.

The next thing we knew, Maxine was happily residing in a brand new private facility. She was getting the right level of care that she could easily afford, and we were paying the bills. So everything worked out for Maxine in the end, but things would have moved a lot smoother and faster with less stress and cost to the public if someone had had power to make decisions about her physical care when she was no longer able to do that herself.

To permit that, Maxine could have signed an advance directive, giving someone power to make decisions about her physical care. This chapter provides a summary of the issues surrounding advance directives. For more information, consult *Living Wills Kit*, another title in the Self-Counsel Press Legal Series.

Advance directives (also known as personal directives) are commonly thought of as living wills; that is, documents for giving specific instructions about the kind of medical treatment you do or do not want to receive at the end of your life. They do that, but they also do something else that may be more important: they let you appoint someone to make sure your instructions are followed.

How many of you could write a list of everything you would want to happen if you were stricken by Alzheimer's tomorrow and were to live for another 10, 20, or even 30 years? What would you say about future medical breakthroughs, about changes in government policies on care for the aging, or about any other unexpected events that could affect your physical and mental well-being? Probably nothing, because you don't know what those things may be.

This brings us back to the realm of the "maybes," and back to the problem of how to plan for them. The answer is simple: don't even try. Instead, appoint someone who knows you, and knows what you value and believe, to look after the maybes for you; someone you trust to make the choices for you that you would have made for yourself. Every province has its own name for that person (refer to Table 5 in the chapter entitled "Estate Planning for Life: The Law of Aging"), but for simplicity, I will use the term health care agent.

The advance directive can be divided into parts (see Table 7). The advance directive, however, does one thing that the other estate planning documents don't do — it tells your agent what you want or do not want if you are at the end of your life because you are terminally ill.

Table 7
THE LOGICAL STRUCTURE OF AN ADVANCE DIRECTIVE

Part	What it does	Underlying question
The setup	Appoints your surrogate financial decision maker (health care agent) and backup	Who will be my agent?
The trigger	Establishes when you have lost capacity and how your agent knows when to take over	When do I want my agent to start?
End-of-life instructions	Tell your agent what end-of-life decisions to make if you are terminally ill	What do I want my agent to do if I am terminally ill?
The attorney's toolbox	Gives your agent power and discretion to handle anypotential occurrences related to your personal and health care (the "maybes")	What does my agent need in order to do the best job?

1. The Setup, or Who Will Be My Agent?

Your health care agent must be someone you trust to follow your wishes about your health care and personal care when you can no longer make those decisions yourself. That implies that the person must know you very well, understand and respect your values and beliefs, and have the strength and courage to ensure that your wishes, values, and beliefs are respected and followed by the outside world. This may or may not be the same person you have already selected for the jobs of executor and attorney. The executor and attorney will handle your assets, but your health care agent will be making personal care decisions that may be very emotional.

However, if you think back to the example of Maxine at the beginning of this chapter, you will remember that the line between estate management and personal care can be a grey one. The best advice is to not leave your loved ones to walk this line. Do all three documents, and even if you can't give them instructions on everything, you will have made it clear who has power to make which type of decision as issues come up.

The most likely candidates for the job of health care agent are spouses, adult children, or close friends, but some people call on clergy or other close advisors. Note that trust companies cannot and will not do this. They are licensed to handle estates, but they do not have the expertise or the legal right to make decisions about personal or health care matters.

Some provinces have another public official, usually called the public guardian, who looks after the personal affairs of incapacitated adults when so ordered by the courts. These officials may be part of the Public Trustee's office (as in Ontario and Manitoba, for example) or they may be found in separate departments (as in Alberta, PEI, NWT, and Nunavut). If you do not do an advance directive, and there is no one to get a guardianship order to look after you, you may eventually come under the care of one of these officials. Also, these public guardians may or may not be willing to accept an appointment as your agent in an advance directive. If you are considering the public guardian option, the best advice is to contact them and ask. Your local public trustee can tell you if there is a public guardian in your province and how to reach them. On the CD you will find contact info for Public Trustees.

2. The Trigger, or When Do I Want My Agent to Start?

The trigger issues are also very similar to the ones we discussed when talking about the enduring power of attorney. You want to make sure no one could possibly abuse your advance directive by making personal care decisions for you when you don't need their help. This can be difficult to determine in many cases. There are many bitter lawsuits between children who don't agree that Mom or Dad has lost capacity to the point where one of them has to take over, and each side will have a medical expert who, in good faith, believes exactly the opposite of his or her colleague on the other side.

So who pulls the trigger? As we saw with enduring power of attorneys, many couples have sufficient trust to allow the other to make this tough call. Others go with their doctor or another health care advisor. There is no perfect answer, so the best advice is to follow your instincts.

3. End-of-Life Instructions, or What Do I Want My Agent to Do If I Am Terminally Ill?

There are two approaches to the issue of end-of-life treatment instructions. You can give your agent —

- General statements based on level of consciousness, degree of suffering, chance of survival, or other quality of life factors.
- Specific treatment choices from a list or written by you, depending on your condition.

Either way, you are trying to be clear about what you do or do not want done to you to keep you alive when faced with a life-threatening illness.

Anything arising from your religious convictions, or anything you learned from an experience with a dying family member or friend can also be included here.

The end-of-life section of the advance directive can be very difficult to write for yourself, so Sample 3: Advance Directive on the CD offers a series of choices you can consider. Select the one that makes the most sense to you. Of course, you are free to make changes, or write your own if you wish.

Most people get to this part of the directive and quit. They just can't wrap their minds around end-of-life choices. I don't blame them, but if that is you, please don't quit. Instead, leave this section out altogether. Then, if these issues come up, your agent will make the best decision he or she can, based on his or her knowledge of your values and beliefs.

4. The Agent's Toolbox, or What Does My Agent Need in Order to Do the Best Job?

If you think of your agent's job in terms of a traditional living will (e.g., to deal only with end-of-life choices), and if your end-of-life instructions are as clear as you can make them, why do you need anything else? The answer lies in the fact that your advance directive is more than a living will — it is designed to give your agent legal power to handle all your personal and health care decisions if you can no longer do that yourself. For that reason I recommend including a list of powers similar to the powers that a judge can give under an adult guardianship order. Those orders have been around for years; they cover most of the typical issues that can arise, and many people are used to dealing with them. These include the power to —

- Make normal health-related decisions, including:
    (i)   obtaining needed treatment, including medical and dental treatment.
    (ii) authorizing admission to or discharge from a facility.
    (iii) consenting to or refusing consent to surgery, medication, therapies, dietary matters, or exercise programs.
    (iv) reviewing medical records.
    (v)   signing documents.
- decide on accommodation and living arrangements, including with whom you will live and associate.
- Decide on social and recreational activities, educational opportunities, and even employment, when relevant.
- Look after legal matters that involve your person (e.g., personal injury claims).

There are a number of other matters you might add, and I refer to these in Sample 3: Advance Directive on the CD. You may want your agent to regularly consult with your friends or family members, or to keep a record of their decisions. You may want your doctor to review your competence on a regular basis. If you are a woman, you may want to say something about what is to be done if you become incapacitated during pregnancy. You may even want to include a paragraph that deals with disputes: I have included a clause in the sample advance directive that directs the agent to try mediation before hiring a lawyer and going to court.

You will also see a clause in the sample advance directive that directs the agent to try to consult with you before making any major decisions. What better way for your agent to show that he or she has your best interests at heart than to ask you what you think? If you are incapacitated and can't communicate at all, no harm done. But if you could communicate — even by a blink of your eye — wouldn't you appreciate being asked?

The sample also contains a number of items I call administrative matters, such as —

- revoking prior advance directives,
- allowing fax copies or photocopies to be as valid as the signed original,
- nominating your advance directive agent as your guardian if there is a court battle,
- releasing from liability those who act on directions from your agent, and
- declaring that your advance directive is to be considered valid in any province where it is needed.

These statements may or may not be legal in every province, but they are a good idea, and they are strong evidence of your intention, which is what this is all about.

Finally, there may even be things you specifically do not want your agent to do, and those can go in, as well. If you are strongly opposed to being kept alive when you have no quality of life, for example, you may want to insert something here about that if you haven't already addressed it in the end-of-life section.

5. The Most Important Person in Your Advance Directive Is Your Agent

Once again, we see that the most important person in this estate-planning document is not you; it is your agent, so pick a good one. All the comments on how to choose an executor and attorney apply here. But there is more. Because your agent will be dealing with very personal issues which can get quite emotional, it goes without saying that he or she should be comfortable with those kind of decisions, and with dealing with all kinds of people. Those you have chosen as your asset managers may or may not be the best ones to select as your health care agent.

Probate Fees and Income

Two topics that always come up in any discussion about wills, and that often drive up people's blood pressure, are the cost of probate and income tax payable at death. Each topic deserves a book of its own, but in the interest of keeping everyone's blood pressure as low as possible, this chapter is going to give you some basic information to think about. For more information on probating an estate see *So You've Been Appointed Executor*, published by Self-Counsel Press.

1. Probate Fees: "I Don't Want My Family to Pay Them"

1.1 What is probate?

The word "probate" comes from the Latin word for "proof." Getting probate is nothing more complicated than proving to a judge that the document that says it is somebody's last will really is. It is a routine legal procedure, so routine that the person applying for probate often doesn't have to appear in front of a judge. Instead, the paperwork is dropped off at the office of the probate clerk, and, if it is in order, the clerk gives it to a probate judge who reviews it, approves it, and signs a probate certificate. This certificate is proof to anyone who needs it that the will is the true last will of the deceased, and that the person it names as executor has full legal power to take charge of the deceased's assets and distribute them as the will directs.

The names of the courts that deal with probate differ from province to province. Consult Table 8 to determine the name of the probate court and laws in your province.

Like executor anxiety, probate anxiety is another little understood psychological condition that was largely unknown in Canada before Ontario dramatically raised its probate fees several years ago. Probate anxiety is characterized by a deep-seated phobia about probate fees, and it is encouraged by an entire probate-avoidance industry that advises people to use any means possible to make sure their hard-earned assets aren't siphoned off in probate fees after they die.

1.2   Fees associated with probate

Three distinct fees are associated with the probate process — even for a routine estate. Strictly speaking, only one of them (the probate tax) is a probate fee, but the others are so closely connected with probate that they are usually lumped together. They are probate tax, legal fees, and executor's fees.

1.2a   Probate tax

Probate tax is the fee charged by the government for processing a probate application through the court.

These fees were previously not considered a tax until an astute woman took the Ontario government to court over them a few years ago. The case is called Re Eurig, and Mrs. Eurig argued that Ontario's probate fees didn't have anything to do with the amount of work involved in processing a probate application. In fact, she said, the fees really amounted to an illegal tax, which the province had disguised as a courthouse processing fee.

She fought her case all the way to the Supreme Court of Canada, and won. But even though this enterprising woman got her fees back, no one

Table 8
PROBATE COURTS AND LAWS BY PROVINCE AND TERRITORY

Province/Territory	Court	Law
Alberta	Queen's Bench	Surrogate Court
British Columbia	Supreme Court	Supreme Court Rules
Manitoba	Queen's Bench	Law Fees Act
New Brunswick	Probate Court	Probate Court Act
Newfoundland	Supreme Court	Rules of the Supreme Court
Northwest Territories	Supreme Court	Probate Rules
Nova Scotia	Probate Court Act	Costs and Fees
Nunavut	Supreme Court	Probate Rules
Ontario	Superior Court of Justice	Administration of Justice Act
Prince Edward Island	Supreme Court	Probate Act
Saskatchewan	Queen's Bench	Queen's Bench Fees Act
Yukon	Supreme Court	Administration of Estates Act

else will — Ontario quickly passed a law making its probate fee a tax, and backdated it to cover every probate fee paid since the end of World War II. Every other province has done the same thing, and their probate fees are now legally a tax. Each province simply confirmed their existing rates, except Alberta, which dropped its rate back to where it was about 25 years ago.

Table 9 shows the current probate tax rates across Canada, based on the total gross value of the estate. Note that Alberta calculates its probate tax on the net value of the estate after debts are subtracted. To get a practical idea of what these rates look like in a typical case, I have calculated the tax in each province on an estate of $500,000. The result is summarized in this table.

Table 9 PROBATE TAX RATES BY PROVINCE AND TERRITORY			
Province/Territory	**Total gross value of the estate**	**Probate tax rate**	**Probate tax on a $500,000 estate**
Alberta (Alberta calculates probate tax on the net value of the estate after debts are subtracted.)	$10,000 or less $10,001 – $25,000 $25,001 – $125,000 $125,001 – $250,000 over $250,001	$25 $100 $200 $300 $400	**$400**
British Columbia	Under $10,000 $10,001 and higher Plus if $25,000 to $50,000 Plus for each $1,000 over $50,001	zero $208 $6 per $1,000 $14 per $1,000	$208 + (25 x $6) + (450 x $14) = **$6,658**
Manitoba	Under $10,000 Plus for each $1,000 over $10,001	$50 $6 per $1,000	$50 + (450 x $6) = **$ 2,750**
New Brunswick	Under $5,000 $5,001 – $10,000 $10,001 – $15,000 $15,001 – $20,000 Plus for each $1,000 over $20,001	$25 $50 $75 $100 $5 per $1,000	$100 + (480 x $5) = **$2,500**

Table 9 — Continued

Newfoundland	Under $1,000
	Plus $0.50 for
	  each $1,000
	  over $1,001
		$60
		+ (499 x $0.50)
		= $309.50
			$60

Northwest Territories	Under $500 $501 – $1,000 Plus for each $1,000 over $1,001	$8 $15 $3 per $1,000	$15 + (499 x $3) = **$1,512**

Nova Scotia	Under $10,000
	$10,001 – $25,000
	$25,001 – $50,000
	$50,001 – $100,000
	over $100,000
	$770 plus $13
	  per each $1,000
	  over $100,000
		$70
		$165
		$275
		$770
			$770
			+ (400 x $13)
			= **$5,970**

Nunavut	Under $500 $501 – $1,000 Plus for each $1,000 over $1,001	$8 $15 $3 per $1,000	$15 + (499 x $3) = **$1,512**
Ontario	Under $1,000 $1,001 – $50,000 plus for each $1,000 over $50,000	Zero $5 per $1,000 $15 per $1,000	(50 x $5) + (450 x $15) = **$7,000**
Prince Edward Island	Under $10,000 $10,001 – $25,000 $25,001 – $50,000 $50,001 – $100,000 Plus for each $1,000 over $100,000	$50 $100 $200 $400 $4 per $1,000	$400 + (400 x $4) = **$2,000**
Saskatchewan	$7 per $1,000	$3,500	
Yukon	Under $10,000 $10,001 – $25,000 Plus for each $1,000 over $25,000	Zero $140 $6 per $1,000	$140 + (475 x $6) = **$2,990**

1.2b Legal fees

Legal fees are the fees charged by lawyers for the legal work involved in the probate application.

Many lawyers prepare the legal documents for a probate application and submit them to the court on behalf of the executor of the estate. The fee they charge for this service used to be set by the government, but this is no longer the case. Today, most lawyers charge by the hour for processing a probate application. However, some may do the work for a fixed fee if the case is routine and there aren't any problems that will complicate the file (such as lawsuits by beneficiaries). If the lawyer's fees seem unreasonable for the amount of work done, you can usually have them reviewed by an independent court officer. Contact your local court for more information.

Some provinces have suggested guidelines for legal fees, but many lawyers are willing to negotiate a fee that is less than the suggested amount. And, of course, if you have the time and energy to get probate without a lawyer, you won't have to pay any legal fees.

1.2c Executor's fees

Executor's fees are the fees payable to the executor for the work he or she does to get probate, and then to settle the estate once probate is issued (also referred to as administration fees).

The Trustee Act of each province and territory says that an executor can claim fair and reasonable compensation for his or her work administering an estate. If the amount claimed by an executor does not seem reasonable to the beneficiaries, then the amount must be reviewed and set by a judge of the appropriate surrogate court. Please note that British Columbia and Prince Edward Island put a maximum limit on the amount an executor can claim for fees. The limit is 5 percent of the estate. This is in line with the amount generally accepted as a rule of thumb for executor's fees, which is 5 percent of the value of the estate, as long as the size of the estate and the amount of work done justify that amount.

If the estate includes setting up and running a trust, then the law allows the executor (or the trustee of the trust if a different person is given that responsibility) to take ongoing fees as follows:

- 2.5 percent of the yearly value of the trust assets and income,
- 2.5 percent of the yearly value of the trust assets disbursed, plus

- 0.4 percent of the yearly average market value of the trust assets as a fee for general care and management of the trust.

Executor's fees must be approved by all the beneficiaries when the executor presents the final accounting before handing over the assets and closing the estate. If the beneficiaries agree with the accounting, they will sign a release allowing the executor to distribute the estate. If a beneficiary objects to the amount the executor is claiming, then they will either have to negotiate, or get the fees approved by a judge. No assets can be distributed until this matter is settled.

There are five factors that a court will look at to make sure that the amount taken for executor's fees is reasonable:

- the size of the estate,
- the care and responsibility required of the executor,
- the amount of time involved in settling the estate,
- the skills and abilities of the executor, and
- the degree of success the executor has in settling the estate quickly, efficiently, and properly.

When the executor is a close family member who is also receiving a share of the estate, he or she will often not claim an executor's fee for the work done in winding up the estate. However, if the estate is complicated — and whenever it is handled by a professional executor such as a trust company — executor's fees will be claimed and paid.

1.2d Other common estate administration costs

A number of other costs don't have anything to do with getting probate, but can come up in the administration of an estate. What they are depends on the assets involved and on how much the executor is willing or able to do himself or herself. For example, if a house must be sold, appraisal fees, realtor's commissions, registry fees, and legal fees for the transfer of title must be paid. And almost every estate needs to file tax returns, which might involve fees payable to an accountant or a tax service.

1.3 Avoiding probate

There are many legitimate ways to structure your affairs to avoid probate. These are beyond the scope of this book and you should consult a lawyer or accountant for more details on this.

2. Income Tax and Death

Until 1972, Canada had a pay-a-percentage-to-the-government type of inheritance tax. This was abolished in 1972 and there is now no inheritance tax in Canada.

However, there most certainly are tax consequences when someone dies. Let's take a brief look at them. Taxation is a complex area, and you or your executor may need detailed, personalized assistance with tax questions from a qualified tax expert.

2.1 Income earned by you to date of death

Just because you die doesn't mean you get out of paying the tax you would have otherwise paid on the taxable income you received while you were still alive. Your executor has to file one last personal tax return for you to catch all your taxable income from January 1 to the date of your death. This is called the T1 terminal return. Your estate does get one break, however: your executor can claim the full calendar year's worth of tax credits for you, no matter when you died.

2.2 Income earned by your estate after death

While your executor is administering your estate, some of your assets are probably earning income. The government knows that and expects its share of tax. Your executor has two choices and he or she should do the calculations and see what is cheaper before making a decision. (**Note:** estates are usually taxed at the same rate as the deceased.) The choices are:

- He or she can pass that income on to your beneficiaries and let them declare their share of it on their tax returns for the year of your death.

- He or she can file a separate return for your estate (called a T3) so that income can be taxed in, and paid out of, your estate. This T3 return covers any income that is not being passed on to beneficiaries from the date of your death to the date your executor winds up the estate.

Your executor must file a separate T3 estate return if one of your beneficiaries is a non-resident of Canada — someone who lives in the United States, for example.

2.3 Capital gains tax at death

When you die, Canada's tax law presumes that, just before death, you sold everything you owned for a fair price (this is called "fair market value"). The tax law then looks at what you paid for your taxable capital assets and subtracts the difference. If those assets went up in value during the time you owned them, that is called a capital gain, and a percentage of that gain is added to your income for the year of your death and is subsequently taxed.

Dealing with capital gains tax at death is a lot simpler than most people think. For many Canadians it may not be relevant at all as the most common capital asset owned by Canadians is their family home, and it is exempt from capital gains tax.

Take, for example, the house Mary and Fred bought after the Second World War. They didn't pay much for it in today's terms, and they know it is worth a lot more if they sold it today. That is what makes the house a capital asset: its value increases over time. The increase in value is called the capital gain, but Mary and Fred won't see a penny of it until it is sold. While tax laws tax the capital gain of other assets, the government doesn't want to penalize Mary and Fred for buying a home. So when they sell it, or when they die, the capital gain on it is not taxable.

However, if you own other capital assets that go up in value, you do pay capital gains tax when those assets are sold or when you die. Let's say that Mary and Fred also owned some shares in Bell Canada. When Fred and Mary die, Canadian tax law tells their executor to follow these three steps in order to determine whether capital gains tax is payable:

(a) Pretend that Fred and Mary sold the Bell Canada shares the second before they died. (This is called a "deemed disposition.")

(b) Determine whether that pretend sale price is higher than the price Fred and Mary paid for the shares when they bought them. (Any increase in price is the capital gain.)

(c) If it is, then add a percentage of that gain to their final T1 terminal returns as income for that year. (This percent is called the inclusion rate, and is currently 75 percent.)

Other commonly owned assets that can trigger a capital gain at death include mutual funds, vacation homes, and non-residential real estate. Cash assets, like term deposits, bank accounts, Canada Savings Bonds, and GICs, are not capital assets because they do not go up in value over time. Instead, they generate income, which is declared and taxed every year.

2.4 Clearance certificate

No discussion of taxes and death is complete without reference to a clearance certificate. A clearance certificate is a letter from Canada Revenue Agency to your executor saying that the government is satisfied that all taxes owing by you or your estate have been properly declared and paid, and the executor may distribute your assets as your will directs.

Every executor wants to know that the government is happy. No executor wants to discover two or three years down the line that there are unpaid taxes owing by the deceased or his or her estate. By then the beneficiaries may have spent their money, and the executor could be dipping into his or her own pocket to cover the shortfall.

Unfortunately, it often takes a while for Canada Revenue Agency to issue clearance certificates. So, once all the tax returns have been prepared and filed, it is common for executors to pay the beneficiaries a portion of their gifts and to hold back the rest until the certificate arrives. Usually, the executor will keep aside double or triple the amount of tax owing as well as any other unpaid amounts such as the executor's fee, just in case Canada Revenue Agency disputes the calculations and more money is owed.

Tax matters can be confusing at the best of times and especially so where estates and trusts are concerned. The best advice is to get good professional advice from a tax specialist, such as a lawyer, accountant, or trust officer.

Finding and Using a Good Wills Lawyer

A note about notaries: In some provinces, such as British Columbia and Quebec, there are both lawyers and notaries. In other provinces lawyers do the work of notaries. If you live in a province where notaries are licensed to do wills, read this section as if it refers to both lawyers and notaries.

1. The Risks of Doing It Yourself

There is no law that says you have to use a lawyer when you create your estate-planning documents. You are free to do any legal documents yourself, and during my 20 years in practice I saw — and successfully probated — a number of do-it-yourself wills. Now and then we had trouble carrying out the instructions. Sometimes the wills were so confusing that the executor had to spend the estate's money getting a judge to decide which of the various possibilities the deceased had in mind, and occasionally the deceased didn't say what was to happen if cousin John died first — but we got probate.

The do-it-yourself approach can work in some situations, but even the so-called "simple will" can go dangerously wrong without input from a lawyer. When you do any legal document yourself you are taking some risks, but as long as you still have full capacity, you can fix most problems if they arise. Unfortunately, estate-planning documents carry a different risk — the risk that you won't be able to fix any problems because by the time they come up you may not have mental capacity anymore, or you may be dead.

The best way I can think of illustrating the risks of doing your own estate-planning documents is to tell you about the advantages and disadvantages of using a lawyer. As you review them, ask yourself if you are comfortable looking after each item yourself. If you are, you are a bona fide "do-it-yourselfer" and should carry on. If not, then the rest of this chapter outlines how to find a good estate-planning lawyer to help you.

2. Advantages of Using a Lawyer

2.1 The "proof you had your marbles" factor

Getting a lawyer to prepare and witness your estate-planning documents, especially if you found the lawyer yourself and met with him or her alone, goes a long way toward establishing the fact that you had full mental capacity when you signed those documents. If you or the lawyer are worried that someone might question that in the future, the lawyer can get a letter from your doctor right away, just in case.

2.2 The "complete advice" factor

A good estate-planning lawyer can give you good local advice on every aspect of your estate plan, and will explain the various documents and how they interrelate. He or she can even give you good information on background issues, such as the different levels of care available in your community and how the public trustee and guardian work in your province. A good lawyer will have contacts with trust companies, accountants, insurance agencies, brokerage houses, and many other professionals working in the expanding elder-care market.

2.3 The "multi-generational thinking" factor

A good estate-planning lawyer will automatically think beyond you and your spouse or companion and ask the "what if" questions that you may not ask yourself: What if your spouse dies before you do? What if your daughter gets married, has children, and gets hit by a bus before you die? What if your son gets divorced? What if one of your grandchildren is handicapped?

2.4 The "who pays if I make a mistake?" factor

If you make a mistake on an estate-planning document yourself, you will have to fix it. If the mistake is found after you are dead, your executor and heirs will have to deal with it. But if you hired and relied on a lawyer, and that lawyer made an error, you or your executor should be able to make a claim against that lawyer's malpractice insurance. If the mistake was due to his or her negligence, your estate should recover the loss.

2.5 The "loss leader" factor

For years many lawyers have treated wills as a loss leader. They would do the will for less than their own cost in the hope that the client would bring in more lucrative business, and that the executor would bring in the estate work after the client died. This attitude still exists in many law practices, so you may get first-class estate planning help for a very reasonable fee.

2.6 The "legal boiler plate" factor

All lawyers have standard clauses that they include as a matter of routine in every estate-planning document. Admittedly, the language used in some of those clauses can be intimidating and difficult to understand, but they often discuss important issues that you might otherwise not think about if you were doing your will without a lawyer.

2.7 The "personal comfort" factor

Most lawyers are in business to solve your problems, not to make them worse. Using a good estate-planning lawyer will go a long way toward giving you the peace of mind that comes from getting a difficult job done well and thoroughly.

2.8 The "future estate work" factor

If you have found a good estate-planning lawyer to do your documents, you have also found a good lawyer to help your family when those documents are triggered. This can be a source of comfort during what is already a stressful time for your family.

3. All Lawyers Are Not Created Equal

For several years when I taught the Alberta Bar admission course on wills, I always began by asking the students, all of whom had law degrees, how many had taken a course on wills at law school. Year after year it never failed — only about half put up their hands. Although the wills course is strongly recommended for anyone going into private practice, it is not compulsory at all law schools.

Most people assume that any lawyer can do a will, and indeed any lawyer can. So people get the lawyer who did their house purchase or their daughter's divorce to do their estate-planning documents. In most cases this works out well, but it's a little like seeing a chiropractor for a heart condition. Many lawyers today are specializing in the area I call the law of aging, and you can be sure that they are up-to-date in the issues surrounding estate planning. Whether you choose to go with a lawyer who has done other legal work for you, or with one that specializes in estate planning, the next section tells you how to be sure the lawyer you choose knows what estate planning is all about.

4. Finding a Good Estate-Planning Lawyer

As in any profession, there are bad lawyers out there, and finding a good estate-planning lawyer will help make the process less painful. A lawyer could be smart and competent, but if he or she (and his or her staff) has no people skills, you could be caught in a nightmare of no phone calls or letters, sloppy drafting, forgotten appointments, and unreadable documents.

A good lawyer will also be up front about fees. All the surveys I've seen on what people don't like about lawyers put fees right near the top — not high fees, but lack of discussion in advance about fees. It's as if some lawyers think the right way to get paid is to present a bill the way they do the Academy Awards: lots of stomach churning suspense, a drum roll, and "the envelope please." If you end up with a lawyer who does that, you haven't followed the advice to finding a good estate-planning lawyer outlined below.

4.1 Get the names of five good lawyers

"Wait a minute!" you say. "That's my problem. I don't know even one good lawyer!" That may be true now, but you are never more than a few phone calls (or maybe even mouse clicks) away from connections with people who deal with lawyers. Those connections fall into two basic groups: public and personal. All you have to do is make a list of your connections. Here's a list to get you started:

Public connections:

- Seniors' organization
- Yellow Pages
- Lawyers' ads
- Lawyer referral services (free ones only)
- Court staff
- Public trustee staff
- Law school professors
- Better Business Bureau

Personal connections:

- Clergy
- Friends from church/synagogue/mosque
- Doctor
- Psychologist
- Social worker
- Public health nurse
- Neighbours
- Parents at your children's school
- Mechanic
- Corner store operator
- Landlord

- People you volunteer with
- People in your night school class

Easy, isn't it? And once you get going you will think of many more.

After you've made a list of people you know who have dealt with lawyers, you need to talk to them. Phone the public connections. Be direct so you don't waste their time, and yours. Ask if they can recommend any good lawyers for estate-planning documents. If they have a policy against that, ask if they can refer you to anyone who can make a recommendation. Then move on.

Talk to your personal connections. Ask them if they have used any lawyers recently. Was it for estate-planning documents or something else? How did it go? Would they recommend him or her? Get names and phone numbers of the lawyers. Keep going until you have five to ten recommended lawyers.

4.2   Use the phone

Once you have your list of five to ten potential candidates, start phoning. Start with the ones you already have a good feeling about. Be ready to speak to a live person — the receptionist — who will most likely tell you the lawyer is not available right now but you can leave a message on his or her voice mail. Don't be put off by this: it's true. The days when you were automatically put through to a lawyer are over, and almost everyone uses technology to manage their time and phone calls. So be ready with a short message for the voice mail. Say you are looking for a lawyer to do your estate-planning documents and ask the lawyer to call you back as soon as possible. Then move on to the next lawyer on your list.

When the lawyer calls back, do some quick weeding. Ask —

- if they do this work;
- if it is a big part of their practice or just a sideline;
- if they attend the Canadian Bar Association's monthly section meetings on wills and estates, or keep up-to-date in another way; and
- if they charge on an hourly basis or have a fixed fee.

The answers to these questions will tell you if the lawyer is focussed on estate planning, or if it is one of a multitude of areas he or she works in. They will also give you a first impression of the person on the other end of the phone, which will go a long way toward telling you whether or not you want to work with this person. The very best answers you are likely to get are —

- "Yes, I do that,"
- "A lot of that,"
- "Yes I keep up with current developments in the area," and
- "That depends."

Don't be upset if the lawyer seems to duck and weave a little on fees. Lawyers are conditioned by years of practice to charge on the basis of the amount of time put in, and they know that first-time clients always underestimate the amount of effort that goes into proper estate planning. That won't be a problem for you because you have read this book, but the lawyer doesn't know that.

In fact, just as you will be listening for certain key words from the lawyer, so will the lawyer be listening for certain key words from you, the most common being, "I just want a simple will." Don't be surprised if that triggers a quick lecture on the realities of estate planning that ends with, " … and in my experience, there really is no such thing as a simple will," or, " … so we may end up with a simple will, but there are a lot of complex issues we have to deal with before we are sure a simple will is the right will for you."

Now make a quick decision. Do you have a good feeling about this person or not? If you do, set up an appointment, and make sure there will be no charge for the first office visit. If you don't like something about how the lawyer talks to you, or if you are uncomfortable with an initial fee, say thanks, hang up, and call the next lawyer on your list until you have two or three office appointments lined up.

4.3 Visit the prospects

When you go to see the two or three prospects you have selected, keep your eyes open. You can learn so much about the person you might be working with just by looking around the waiting room. Is the reception area neat and tidy? Does someone speak to you or are you left on your own? How long is the wait? Is there any estate planning or elder law information on display? Brochures? Magazines? Articles? What about samples of the work they do? Is there a sample will, enduring power of attorney, or advance directive in a binder for you to look over? Are their business cards crisp or tattered, dull or interesting?

When you are seated in the lawyer's office what do you see? Desk and cabinets piled high with files? Boxes labelled "Confidential — Jones Accident" in the corners? Or is it tidy and organized? Does the lawyer take an obvious interest in your needs, or does he or she launch into a speech using jargon and language you don't understand? Do you get the feeling the lawyer is watching the clock, or does he or she give you enough time to tell your story and ask questions? Are your questions answered to your satisfaction? Is the basis for charging the fee made clear?

You may want to make notes during this visit so you don't have to rely entirely on your memory later. When the meeting is over, tell the lawyer that you are meeting with some other lawyers and you hope to make your choice as soon as you can. As a lawyer, I always made notes during these sessions and kept them in a file labelled "potential new clients." If I didn't hear back in a couple of weeks, I would throw them out. You may want to say that if you decide to go with that lawyer you will call, otherwise he or she can assume you went somewhere else.

After visiting two or three lawyers, you should have a pretty good idea if you can work with any one of them. If so, pick one, call, and make the next appointment. Then, control the passage of time. I blush to say it, but I know from experience that legal work has a way of expanding to fill the time available. To prevent that, I always tried to give clients a fixed date when they would hear from me next and write it down. If I couldn't make it, I tried to phone them before the deadline to explain why and set a new one. People don't like delay, but they prefer to find out about it ahead of time rather than have a deadline go by and then wait, and wait, and wait to hear something.

If you didn't find a lawyer you could work with the first time, don't give up. Go back to gathering more names of lawyers (see section 4.1) and repeat the process. With some careful selection, you'll find the right person to help you plan your estate.

Basic Will and Worksheets

Basic Will

THIS IS THE LAST WILL of me, _____ ,

[your full legal name],

of _____ , Canada

[city or town and province or territory],

PART I — INITIAL MATTERS

REVOCATION

I revoke all former Wills and Codicils.

EXECUTORS AND TRUSTEES

[insert the executor clause you chose in Step 1 here]

My Trustees may pay themselves a reasonable fee for the work they do, in addition to any gift or benefit that I leave them in this Will, provided that the amounts are either

a.   approved by the Surrogate Court; or

b.   approved by all of the beneficiaries of my estate.

SURVIVORSHIP

Any beneficiary who is not alive thirty (30) clear days after my death is considered not to have survived me.

DISPOSITION OF MY BODY

I direct that my body be disposed of as my Trustees see fit.

PART II — DISPOSITION OF ESTATE

I give all my property, including any property over which I have a general power of appointment, to my Trustees on the following trusts:

PAYMENT OF DEBTS

To pay —

all my legally enforceable debts,

my funeral expenses, and

the expenses incurred in administering my estate.

DISTRIBUTION OF RESIDUE

To transfer the residue of my estate to
   [insert the distribution clause you selected in Step 3 here]

PART III — POWER TO ADMINISTER MY ESTATE

To carry out the terms of my Will I give my Trustees the following powers:

EXERCISE OF PROPERTY RIGHTS

My Trustees may exercise any rights that arise from ownership of any property of my estate. This includes the right to conduct any legal actions necessary with respect to the estate property.

REALIZATION AND SALE

To realize and sell my estate assets on terms my Trustees think advisable. They may delay conversion until it is advantageous. They can hold assets in the form that they are in at my death even if the assets are not approved for Trustees. They will not be responsible for any loss which may occur from a properly considered decision to leave investments in the form that they were in when I died.

PAYMENTS TO BENEFICIARY

To make any payment for a person younger than the age of majority to *[his or her]* parent or guardian and the receipt of that parent or guardian will be a sufficient discharge to my Trustees.

DISTRIBUTION IN KIND

To transfer the assets of my estate to my beneficiaries without converting them into cash when that is reasonable. For this purpose my Trustees will determine the value of the assets involved and their valuation will be binding.

INVESTMENTS

If I live in a jurisdiction that restricts Trustee investments to a prescribed list, to invest my estate assets in investments that are not authorized for Trustees.

TAX ELECTIONS

To make any elections available under the Income Tax Act of Canada or any other applicable statute.

EMPLOYMENT OF AGENTS

To employ any agent to carry out the administration of my estate and its trusts.

APPORTIONMENT OF RECEIPTS

To decide whether receipts are income or capital in their discretion.

ENCROACHMENT POWER

Except as otherwise provided in this Will, if my Trustees hold any share of my estate in trust they shall have the power to spend as much of the income or capital or both as my Trustees consider advisable for the maintenance, education, advancement, or benefit of the beneficiary of that trust.

RESOLUTION OF DISPUTES

If any disputes should arise regarding:

> the administration of my estate,

> the interpretation of this Will, or

> any other matter connected with my estate,

I give my Trustees power to retain the services of any competent mediator or arbitrator, as they see fit. It is my intention that the costs of resolving any disputes be kept to an absolute minimum and that litigation be used only as a last resort.

BORROWING

To borrow money for the estate with or without security.

REAL PROPERTY

To manage, sell or lease any real property in my estate on such terms as they choose and to spend such amounts as may be necessary to maintain and repair it.

CORPORATE AND BUSINESS ASSETS

To represent my estate as a shareholder in any corporations in which it holds shares and to participate in any corporate decisions required.

To carry on any business I was engaged in as if I were still alive.

To incorporate a company to carry on any business or hold any assets of my estate.

RENEWAL OF GUARANTEES

To renew any Guarantees or Securities I may have given to secure the debt of another person and to renew them only for the purpose of an orderly liquidation. I direct my Trustees to do this without undue embarrassment to my family or business associates.

SIGNATURE OF TESTATOR

I, _____
                   [your full legal name]

have subscribed my name to this my Will

on the _____ day of _____, _____
         [day]   *[month]*   *[year],*

at the _____ of _____
       [City or town]   *[name of city or town]*

in the Province of _____

_____
X *[Sign here using your normal signature].*

SIGNATURES OF WITNESSES

Signed by _____ as _____ will,
        [full legal name of the testator]   *[his/her]*

in our presence and attested by us in _____ presence
                       [his/her]

and in the presence of each other

_____
          [Signature of witness 1]

Name: _____
           [Print or type name of witness 1]

Address: *[Witness 1]*

_____

_____

_____

_____
          [Signature of witness 2]

Name: _____
           [Print or type name of witness 2]

Address: *[Witness 2]*

_____

_____

_____

[make sure the signatures of the will maker and both witnesses are on the same page, that they all sign at the same time, and they see each other sign.]

WORKSHEET 1
STEP 1: CHOOSE YOUR EXECUTOR CLAUSES

Select the clause you require:

	Sole executor with alternate
	Joint executors with substitute
	Public Trustee or Trust Company

Note: If choosing the Public Trustee or a Trust Company, always contact them first for any specific clauses they require.

WORKSHEET 2
STEP 2: CATEGORIZE YOUR PROPERTY

Your Asset Information:

Category 1: Your Non-Estate Assets

1.1   **Joint assets with right of survivorship:**

Joint real estate:

Name of co-owner _____

Address _____

Legal description _____

Type: (check these as appropriate)

     [   ]   House

     [   ]   Cottage

     [   ]   Farm

     [   ]   Condo

     [   ]   Acreage

     [   ]   Rental property

     [   ]   Commercial property

     [   ]   Leases (e.g., apartment, office, mineral rights)

     [   ]   Bare, undeveloped land

Joint cash assets:

Co-owner _____

Financial institution _____

Address _____

Account number _____

Location of papers _____

Type: (check as appropriate)

     [   ]   Joint bank accounts

     [   ]   Canada savings bonds

     [   ]   Term deposits

     [   ]   Guaranteed income certificates

Other Joint Investments:

Stocks or shares

     Co-owner _____

     Issuing company _____

     Location of certificate _____

Mutual funds
    Co-owner _____
    Issuing company _____
    Who to contact _____

1.2   Designated beneficiary assets

Life insurance products:

Life insurance policy
    Company _____
    Policy number _____
    Location of papers _____
    Name of beneficiary _____
        Address _____
        Phone number _____

Segregated mutual funds
    Account number _____
    Contact info _____
    Name of beneficiary _____
        Address _____
        Phone number _____

Registered plans:

Registered Retirement Savings Plan (RRSP)
    Financial institution _____
    Plan number _____
    Name of beneficiary _____
        Address _____
        Phone number_____

Registered Retirement Income Fund (RRIF)
    Financial institution _____
    Plan number _____
    Name of beneficiary _____
        Address _____
        Phone number _____

Locked In Retirement Account (LIRA)

    Financial institution _____

    Account _____

    Name of beneficiary _____

        Address _____

        Phone number _____

Employment Pensions:

    Employer _____

    Plan administrator _____

    Address _____

    Phone number _____

    Name of beneficiary _____

        Address _____

        Phone number _____

Category 2: Your Estate Assets

2.1   Assets in your name only

Real estate:

    Address _____

    Legal description _____

    _____

    Check as appropriate:

        [   ]   House

        [   ]   Cottage

        [   ]   Farm

        [   ]   Condo

        [   ]   Acreage

        [   ]   Rental property

        [   ]   Commercial property

        [   ]   Lease (e.g., apartment, office, mineral rights)

        [   ]   Bare, undeveloped land

Cash accounts:

    Account number _____

    Financial institution _____

    Branch address _____

    Branch phone number _____

Investments:

Financial institution _____

Account number _____

Personal property of value:

Vehicles:

make, model, year _____

Collections (itemize) _____

_____

Tools (itemize) _____

_____

Family heirlooms or other items of unusual emotional value

_____

_____

Debts owing to you:

By family members (details) _____

By others (details) _____

_____

2.2   Joint as tenant in common assets

Real estate:

Address _____

Legal description _____

_____

Check as appropriate and give the name and address of the other joint tenant and your share of ownership for each:

[   ]   House _____

[   ]   Cottage _____

[   ]   Farm _____

[   ]   Condo _____

[   ]   Acreage _____

[   ]   Rental property _____

[   ]   Commercial property _____

[   ]   Lease (e.g., apartment, office, mineral rights) _____

_____

[   ]   Bare, undeveloped land _____

Cash accounts:

    Account number _____

    Financial institution _____

    Branch address _____

    Branch phone number _____

    Name and address of other tenant in common _____

    _____

    Your share of ownership _____

Investments:

    Financial institution _____

    Account number _____

    Name and address of other tenant in common _____

    _____

    Your share of ownership _____

Other (give details):

    _____

    _____

    _____

    _____

    _____

    _____

    _____

    _____

WORKSHEET 3
STEP 3: CHOOSE YOUR DISTRIBUTION CLAUSE

Review the distribution clauses provided and put a check mark beside the one that best applies to you:

Couples with children

	Married opposite-sex couple with children
	Unmarried or common-law opposite-sex couple with children
	Married same-sex couple with children
	Unmarried same-sex couple with children

Couples without children

	Married opposite-sex couple without children
	Unmarried or common-law opposite-sex couple without children
	Married same-sex couple without children
	Unmarried same-sex couple without children

Singles

	Single person with children
	Single person without children

More great titles from Self-Counsel Press!

Ask for these titles at your local bookstore or visit our website at *www.self-counsel.com*

CD Contents

The following blank forms are included for your use on the attached CD-ROM in Word and PDF formats.

Basic Forms

- Basic Will
- Step 1: Choose Your Executor
- Step 2: Identify Your Property

Samples

- Step 3: Choose Your Distribution Clauses ("samples" folder with 10 sample clauses included)

Advanced Forms

These are the forms from the Resources section of this book:

- Will with Alternate Distribution Clause
- Enduring Power of Attorney
- Advance Directive

Bonus Forms

These are bonus forms that you may need when organizing your property:

- Vehicles and Vessels
- People to Contact
- Property and Real Estate
- Contents of House
- Storage, Safety Deposit Boxes and Safes
- Money Owed to Me
- Storage of Documents
- Checklist of Things to Be Done When a Death Occurs